"PLEASE SIR! / 'EYY ROBERT!"

THE TEACHER

Don Roberts

BALBOA.
PRESS
A DIVISION OF HAY HOUSE

Balboa Press books may be ordered through booksellers or by contacting:

Balboa Press
A Division of Hay House
1663 Liberty Drive
Bloomington, IN 47403
www.balboapress.com.au
1 (877) 407-4847

Print information available on the last page.

ISBN: 978-1-5043-1424-4 (sc)
ISBN: 978-1-5043-1425-1 (e)

Balboa Press rev. date: 08/20/2018

CONTENTS

AUTHOR'S COMMENT

I write this book in the hope that it might benefit those who read it, particularly teachers in training and young teachers in the early stages of their careers. In no way do I claim that I had all the answers, or that this is the way all teachers should teach in this present modern era.

What I do say, is that I believe that all teachers should formulate their aims as a teacher clearly in their minds, and construct a philosophy, or a plan of action that will best achieve those aims. My hope is that by reading my philosophy, they might gain an idea or two, or perhaps even more, that might work for them, and inspire them to prepare a philosophy of their own.

The philosophy, as expressed in the following pages seemed to work well for me.

Although it was unfortunately cut short, I loved every day of my teaching career, and wish all teachers well in their teaching experiences.

I would also like to take this chance of thanking those who helped in the production of this book.

I refer to my butcher Paul (Bluey) Mills who has once again drawn the excellent cartoons, and to Chris Tobin, principal of Merrimac High School for graciously agreeing to write the following most insightful foreword.

Although I originally regarded my reading target for this book to be teachers, teachers in training, and those who might be considering teaching as their future occupation, I feel that any person interested in the education of children, particularly the parents of children attending school, or soon to be attending school, will find it to provide interesting reading.

****

FOREWORD

I first met Don as a student at Merrimac State High School. Of course, that statement is not as it first appears to be. He is a very willing student of the University of the Third Age, an organisation epitomising the concept of lifelong learning. Don engages both as a learner and a teacher, playing an important role in this growing community of learners.

He had just finished his previous book and we were reminiscing about the challenges and joys of teaching in small rural locations. I remember at the conclusion of the conversation thinking how, even in Don's retirement, he was passionately committed to the belief that great teaching delivers life changing opportunities. The flame still burns within Don to teach, to help others learn and guide them towards leading fulfilling lives.

In this book, Don shares his wisdom of a teaching lifetime and distils these experiences into a personal 14 point philosophy of teaching.

While some might want to skip to the page that captures the 14 points, such an exercise would entirely miss the worth of this book. A google search of "10 most powerful teaching philosophies" would be much quicker and returns 3,780,000 results; a literature search of education texts would also reveal countless teaching philosophies. However, neither of these methods have taken a lifetime to develop or are placed contextually within the everyday life of a teacher. Skipping to only the philosophies, and not taking the time to be immersed in the context, you will lose much of the book's beauty. Similar to the Sergeant Major Headmaster's teaching of poetry; fully explained in the book.

Don's stories emphasise over and over again, the importance of developing strong, robust, and professional relationships with all your students. If there is one cornerstone upon which great teaching is built it surely must be the quality of the relationship between teacher and student. This has been a universal truism from the time of Aristotle until today. I often discuss with our teaching staff how fortunate we are as teachers to be one of the few groups in society paid to have strong, engaging, and professional relationships with adolescents. It is through these relationships that great teachers take their students from the known to the unknown, and students achieve what they first thought impossible.

However, this relationship can be even richer when parents are active partners with teachers. Whether it be parents in cities, rural towns or even on a Pacific island, it is difficult to find a parent who does not want their child to achieve more in life than they have achieved. Don outlines the challenges he has faced, the joy he has celebrated, and the lifelong friendships made by partnering with parents. He also gives a few tips for when parents behave badly.

Another highlight of the book is when the students in the one-teacher rural school were found chasing down a goanna. (Might I say, a common activity for bush kids, of which their city counterparts would be terrified.) Don draws on this example to explain the quality of the teacher/student relationship, but also how great learning can be drawn from such experiences. Today, most teachers, whatever the learning environment, should be on the lookout for such opportunities. However, great teachers ruthlessly exploit these experiences to create learning that will be remembered for a lifetime. At Merrimac High, using our pedagogical language, it would be called "enacting on the spot". It is this ability that distinguishes a teacher from a trainer. The teacher is meticulously prepared but will take the risk to abandon their plans when they identify an even more engaging learning opportunity. It is this instantaneous decision making that both challenges and rewards great teachers. The ability to "enact on the spot" is also a cornerstone for great teachers.

The role of the teacher is complex and challenging.

Much of the complexity comes from the challenges of fast-paced lives, overscheduling, and complex family situations. Societal expectations on schools, and therefore teachers, have never been as demanding. Commensurately, teacher training programs have been increased to a five-year Master's degree covering much needed educational theory, child and adolescent development and cognitive learning. However, at the heart of all teacher training will always be practical experience. A great deal of time and money go into matching experienced teachers with developing teachers. Teaching is an art form which has at its core the master/apprentice relationship. Practice and experience will always be needed to complement theoretical studies. The lessons to be learnt, by not only apprentice but also the master, are contextually very well documented in Don's book. Don's story of his lifetime of teaching captures what he has learnt over all these years. More importantly, it confirms he has one of the finest traits of a great teacher: to be an expert learner.

A learner that never stops wondering what else there is to be learnt. 'EYY Robert – well done!

Chris Tobin
Principal
Merrimac State High School
Gold Coast
Australia
2018

CHAPTER 1

SCHOOL DAYS 1939 - 1950

At the tender age of eight, I made an irrevocable decision to become a teacher – not just any teaching role, but the teacher of a school in the bush, where I could also live on a farm. Such was my determination to stick to that as my future, that I knocked back other rather tempting futures in career and sport, and lost a long-term girlfriend, as her intentions appeared to place a stumbling block in the way of achieving that ambition.

One of three boys, who were proving to be quite a handful for our pregnant mother, I was sent away from my Melbourne home to live for three months with my Auntie Marj and Uncle Bill. They lived in a teacher's residence attached to his one-teacher school, in the sparsely populated dairying district of Dollar in the South Gippsland area of Victoria.

Every year we spent a week in the country town of Castlemaine with my grandmother and two maiden aunts, a week that was far and away the highlight of my year, but this was heaven – three whole months of blissful existence. Uncle Bill and Auntie Marj had two children of their own, as well as we three waifs. What a wonderful couple they must have been! I can't remember a cross word spoken - everything seemed to run smoothly and without fuss. I even remember having to clean my shoes on Saturday night ready for church on Sunday, so that no unnecessary chores were done on the Lord's Day – I didn't even consider complaining.

Each day at school seemed fun. No-one shouted or became cranky with me, and I always seemed to be busy either doing my work or helping another kid, which was allowed, even encouraged. Uncle Bill never seemed to get upset, and treated us like his larger family. Compared to the school life back home in Melbourne, where I was often bored with not enough work, or work that was too easy and held no interest, this school was a continuous joy.

Early every morning I would set off on foot with a billy in my hand to collect the day's supply of fresh milk from the nearest dairy farm – quite a walk, but I looked forward to it immensely, and never had to be asked twice. The cheerful banter of the milk-shed intrigued me. One man, while he was milking, would squirt a stream of warm milk into my mouth, or at least some of it went in, with the rest finishing all over my face. This became a daily highlight routine. On the way to and from the farm, I revelled in the peaceful countryside, and marvelled at how the cows grazed contentedly on extremely steep hillsides. Did they perhaps have extension legs for such situations?

"Eight was a very young age to decide your future," you may think. It probably was, and particularly for a child like me.

At home, I had developed a reputation of getting up to mischief, particularly at school, but also to a degree in my neighbourhood. For the whole three months of my stay at Dollar, I never even considered stepping out of line – life was too much fun, no-one fussed, I was expected to do the right thing and it seemed perfectly normal to do so. My uncle was most probably an excellent teacher, although, at that time I was too young to appreciate the fact. Everyone seemed happy, we were busy, and I don't remember him ever needing to raise his voice. I hated teachers shouting.

A few memories still stay with me from this blissful period of my life.

One is Queenie. Queenie was the large, old, totally placid horse, that brought the four children of a farming family to school every day. She was also rather over-weight, as she never changed her gait from a slow walk, and served as a mower, spending the whole day grazing contentedly and totally unfettered on the lush grass of the large school-ground. She would appear every day, well on time, with these four little bodies lined up on her back. The oldest child sat second from the front with the rather unnecessary reins loosely grasped in one hand, and the other arm encircling the youngest. The other two, in order of size, were seated behind him. Due to the size of the children in relation to

Queenie's girth, the oldest lad's legs were the only pair that managed to hang towards the ground a little. All the legs of her other three riders, were forced to be spread horizontally above either flank. It was a sight that never failed to bring a broad grin to my face every morning.

At recess and lunch breaks, we would all try to ride Queenie. The school ground table with its bench seats made a most suitable mounting aid. Queenie would allow herself to be led to our mounting area, despite the fact she must have known her fate. One after the other we would mount. If she felt that too many had climbed on, she would just fold her forelegs and lower her head to the ground, invariably causing us to slide gently over her head. At times, I would pretend she was a bucking bronco and I the intrepid buckjump jockey. The power and extent of the child imagination is without bounds. As a teacher in later years, I took full advantage of that innate talent.

Although I was obviously far too young to realise it at the time, I believe also that my philosophy of teaching also began to take seed at that school. Shouting at children and having temper tantrums was obviously counter-productive, and children should be constantly occupied and challenged. As well as those elements, school should be fun – far more learning surely takes place if children are happy, even laughing.

From that day, nothing swayed my determination. I decided then and there that I would either be a farmer, or a teacher in a small country school. Due to financial constrictions, the latter won the day.

Meanwhile, after arriving home again, I quickly slipped back into my old routine. Soon the shouting teachers became a common occurrence, once again the fun element of the classroom was missing, and I was soon again bored by the ease, and lack of any challenge presented to me therein. Almost immediately I concentrated on two of my better talents, sport and mischief.

I had arrived at the school on my first day, consumed by enthusiasm and anticipation. If the teacher asked a question of the class, I would wave my arm furiously, and edge my way down the aisle in the desperate hope of being chosen to answer. Probably my enthusiasm was too extreme, obviously not appreciated, and was so firmly discouraged that it quickly evaporated. Before long, it became clear to me that schoolwork was boring and too easy, offering me no challenge. With my enthusiasm now totally evaporated, my attention turned to the three other areas at which I excelled.

The Art of Love-making.

The first of these was romance, the second was inventing forms of mischief, and the third was playing sport.

I had a clear understanding of the technique of love-making. Boy chases screeching girl all around the school-ground, but doesn't quite catch her. After all, what would you do if you did catch her? When girl has attracted enough attention for enough onlookers to realise how tantalizing she is to boys, she heads for the sanctity of the girl's dunny. She then gives cheek from the dunny entrance, disappearing into the dunny whenever boy threatens to approach, knowing he does not dare to enter therein. The thrill of love-making soon paled, however, so other forms of mischief had to be investigated, and the limited sport available in the infant school playground played. I could not wait to go up to the big kids' school when I reached Gr 3, as cricket equipment and footballs were distributed for school-ground play.

My reputation as a difficult child was originally forged early in my Gr 2 year. Interestingly it was all due to one of my greatest lifetime achievements. The boys' toilet was attached to an outside school wall and did not boast a roof. Above the urinal was a brick wall, always dripping with small boy urine, as we all desperately attempted to "piss over the dunny wall." Eventually, after twelve months dedicated training, I succeeded. Dreadfully disappointed that no other kid was there to witness my amazing feat, I none-the-less let out a triumphant yell. Even more did I regret my lack of an audience when my triumph was dramatically cut short by the sudden rampaging arrival of a furious infant mistress. Though I quickly holstered my weapon and put on my most innocent expression, it was of no use. The total lack of other possible suspects indisputably stamped me as guilty, thus I was towed by one ear, with my feet on tippy toes hardly touching the ground, to the dreaded crossed line outside the office. There I was forced to stand for hours, ridiculed by all passers-by, awaiting the punishment of the heavy ruler whacking my dancing legs. The glorious thought that just maybe I had scored a bull's eye, bolstered me, helping me to survive the ordeal.

Triumph! Whoops, Trouble!

5

This naughty boy reputation was regularly stoked throughout my primary years, culminating with activities like competitions with Bill, my partner in crime, to see who could earn the strap the most times in a week. At twelve each by one Thursday lunchtime, I recall that we called it a draw, so our hands wouldn't be too sore for Friday afternoon sport.

That mischief was never spiteful, nor did it ever involve bullying. I hated bullying, from which I fortunately didn't personally suffer, and all my life I have done everything in my power to prevent it. Being older I could make sure it didn't happen to my younger brother, and when my older brother, Ken, became a victim, I decided to do something about it. Ken's problem was that he was far too clever for his own good. Already rather young for his grade, he had been required to complete grades 1 and 2 in one year, which made him by far the baby of year 3. Academically he was still fine, but due to his age, he struggled socially, having only one friend, who was also rather a social misfit. Luckily, his situation changed for him to enjoy a wonderful teenage.

I was in Gr 4 when the two oversize bullies of the school started to target him. Realising that he had no answer to the bullying, and that it was making his life at school utterly miserable, I decided that something had to be done. Alone I could do nothing, but by surrounding myself with the twenty other boys in my class, I created a formidable midget army. With screeching threats and wild war cries, we twenty-one descended 'en masse on the two bullies. Bullies are renowned as being cowards. These two proved to be no exception, and fled before our frightening onslaught. They were forced to climb over the school fence to escape our threat, which resulted in them being caught by the teacher on yard duty, and punished for being out of bounds. What a triumph!

Our project succeeded in that the bullying of Ken ceased from that day. Unfortunately for me, it was transferred from him to me. Being fast on my feet and very alert to the danger, I managed to avoid their attempts for three weeks. However, they were determined to wreak their vengeance, so there was an inevitable end. Eventually, Dimmer, the hit man of the pair, cornered me as I was putting my lunch rubbish in the incinerator behind the shelter shed.

"Got you!" he unnecessarily announced. I was well aware of that fact, as my head was already locked in his signature headlock.

The Bully Sets to Work.

"Let's see how good you are without your army of brats!" he triumphantly continued, as he began pummelling me mercilessly. Quite helpless in that awkward position, my arms flailed utterly ineffectively. Obviously, I could not survive this punishment for long.

As invariably happens when a school-ground fight begins, numerous children quickly saw the event, and charged towards the struggle, shouting, "Fight! Fight!"

Fortunately for me, the teacher I admired the most during my school life, Mr White, the school sports-master, was the teacher on yard duty at the time. Quick to act, he arrived on the scene and separated us. He would have known all about me for two reasons. Firstly, I'm sure other teachers would have bitterly complained of my behaviour, and secondly, he would regularly come down to the cricket nets or the football area at recess times to watch. Often, he would join in our play, offering advice to his present school team players and assessing the possibilities of prospects for future teams. Due to being so much smaller and younger than all the other boys participating, I would no doubt have caught his attention. I'm sure he would also have known all about the two school bullies.

"Now boys," he said in a no-nonsense tone, "if you have a disagreement you should solve it like gentlemen, with a properly conducted boxing bout, refereed, and conducted according to the Marquis of Queensbury Rules."

Sending a responsible boy for two pairs of boxing gloves, he led us into the shelter-shed. The shed walls nearly burst with the hordes of onlookers that crowded into it, all barracking loudly before the bout even started. To my delight, without exception, they were all cheering for me. Bullies may be treated with awe, but are invariably disliked by most children.

"Hit him, Don!" they shouted

"Give him one in the snout for me!" I heard, knowing well that request was to me.

So many other gems of advice came tumbling out from countless voices, the enthusiastic yells almost lifting the roof.

With him being unable to use his far superior strength, I proved to be much too fast for the lumbering bully. Also, I had recently attended a gymnasium, which had just finished a three-month course of boxing lessons, culminating in a boxing tournament, which I had won. Thus, I had the knowledge and was high on confidence. Gleefully appreciated by the yelling audience, I gave him what appeared to be a thorough thrashing, landing with about thirty punches to his one successful blow. Mr White and I were probably the only ones who noticed that my punches were as effective as tapping him with a powder puff, and his one punch probably hurt me more than my many blows hurt him.

However, I was never again bullied, and, in fact, to my knowledge very little bullying occurred in the school ground for some time.

Maybe Mr White's methods might not be recommended, or even prove acceptable to present day authorities, and I admit that I never actually adopted that specific solution to bullying myself. However, not only were they effective, but nearly fifty later, at a school reunion, he was constantly surrounded by numerous appreciative ex-pupils, several of whom, including me, he remembered by name, despite the school having had eleven hundred pupils, and all those intervening years.

Only three teachers exerted unquestionable control over me during my primary school years, each using quite different methods. Miss Davies, in Grade 6 terrified me. She achieved this by totally humiliating me once in front of all my classmates, and leaving me in no doubt that this would be repeated each and every time I even thought of stepping out of line. Although I can't remember my misdemeanour that caused her ire, it cannot have been sufficiently bad to earn such treatment. Wearing large, fine-rim spectacles, with a round red face and straight hair cut square and short, she presented a severe, even formidable appearance. As a result of whatever the crime I had committed, I was made to stand on the platform in front of the class, while she delivered her own particular form of punishment. She forced me to sing solo, a pathetic song, which began with,

"If I had a donkey and it would not go,
Do you think I'd smack him? Oh no, no, no, no."

The quality of those ridiculous words did not improve at all during the rest of the song.

As if this were not bad enough for a small boy, she held me firmly by one arm with one of her strong chubby hands all through the song, while she whacked me constantly with her fifteen-inch ruler, on the back of my wildly dancing legs as I tried to sing. Throughout the whole performance, she kept shouting, "Sing, you wretched child!"

On several occasions, I faced six cuts of the strap from strong men, without flinching, or shedding a single tear, but I cried my eyes out from the sheer mortification and humiliation of Miss Davies' furious punishment.

It worked. I was a model of behaviour when involved with her. However, such a method of control was indelibly etched into my teaching philosophy as a most definite no-no!

The thought of misbehaving never entered my mind during the science classes with Miss Devine, for the simple reason that I liked her. Why I liked her I may not have been able to put into words at that time, but I feel it was because she always, spoke quietly, she looked at me and listened intently when I wished to talk to her, and she smiled at me, as if she were fond of me. That description leaves me with no need to elucidate further on what *she* added to my theories of teaching.

Mr White was everything I wanted to become. He was interested in his pupils and was quite prepared to go the extra mile to help us. He, like Miss Devine, gave you his full attention. I loved the way he would often leave the comforts and company of the staff room to play with us in the yard during recesses, before school and at lunch breaks, and he would happily conduct a conversation with us. The many extra hours he put in to train us seemed to be ungrudgingly given. In fact, his enthusiasm indicated that he enjoyed working with us.

Reflecting later, on my primary school years, though perhaps with a little bias, I felt that my constant tendency to find myself in deep trouble was due more to the other teachers' attitudes and methods of teaching, rather than by me being incorrigible. At Sunday school, I had been a model child and loved every minute I spent there. For this I give credit to those wonderful people who volunteered to teach there. Miss Kirwin won my affection when I heard my father apologise for my loud tuneless singing wrecking her kindergarten anniversary item.

"Oh Earle!" she replied. "You have no cause to apologise for Don. He's my best singer." She explained that because I sang with confident enthusiasm in a loud voice, all the frightened little children, who could sing in tune, gained confidence from me, which ensured our item's success.

At age eight I had old Mr Allen who looked more like Father Christmas than Santa himself. No matter how early we arrived, he was there waiting for us, his large body sprawled on the front pew. He listened and chuckled as we climbed all over him, pouring out all our thoughts and telling him of our deeds.

Mrs Fanny Ward was one of those rare people who loved, and was loved, by everyone. She hugged anyone from babies to geriatrics. To my good fortune, she taught me the following year. She would only teach *her boys,* as she called us, as she claimed boys were more fun than girls. If she felt the lesson was too boring, she would ignore it, and make up some interesting story involving ships or planes or something exciting for boys. I'm not sure what they contributed to our religious education, but her love certainly influenced us. As I reached my teens I experienced two brilliant teachers in the youth discussion groups. Both had the knack of firing us up by making utterly outrageous statements with seemingly serious expressions. Against these statements, we would vigorously argue. My state schoolteachers could have learned lots from these untrained, but well-meaning, insightful volunteers.

My final year at central school, year 8 or form two, was important to my future. Of course, I could not be made a school prefect, as the teachers, who would obviously be unimpressed by my behaviour record, chose all the prefects. However, I did become one of the four house captains, who were elected by the children. I also became the first child ever from the school, to make a Victorian State Representative sport squad, achieved as a cricketer. This recognition and responsibility did not magically change me from the problem child to the angel, but it did start the process. I lead my house with diligence, won the best handwriting award for the whole school, because it gained points for my house, and performed particularly well for the two secondary school teachers I liked. Debating also sparked my interest, resulting in me becoming the lead speaker for one of the two Form 2 debating teams. Interestingly my partner in crime and best friend, Bill, became the leader of the other team. Over the years, we had loved competing against each other in sport, and mischief making. Perhaps surprisingly to our teachers, we enjoyed the mental competition of the debating as much as any of our previous physical competitions. For most other teachers, I modified my behaviour a little, but remained a considerable problem for two, whom I regarded as having no right to attempt to teach us.

At the end of the year I gained respectable results in most subjects, excellent ones in subjects I liked, but had my first ever failure - a very poor result in French. This was due to the fact that my French teacher probably should never have become a teacher. She had no rapport whatsoever with children, and consequently no classroom control, a situation over which I took full advantage. This, of course, proved of great detriment to my results. Our school was a feeder school for a prestigious high school, but to gain entry, boys were required to sit for an entrance exam. Sadly, I would be unable to attend this secondary school, as to even qualify to sit the entrance exam, you had to have passed in every subject in your final primary year.

Enter Mr White, who had taught me English and been my sports master. He also taught a French class – I wished I had been in that class. He gave me the chance to sit a supplementary exam, which he conducted, but to no avail. I just hadn't learned any French. As I watched, totally ignored and anxiously waiting, he marked my paper – no facial expression showed to give me a clue. Eventually he looked up and called me to his table.

"I can find no way to give this paper more than a mark of 37, which is a shame, as you cannot attend this excellent high school without a pass mark."

After pausing for this to take effect, he added, "However, if I should add two marks to each question you would score 51."

I stood frozen waiting. After a considerable pause, he relieved my tension by adding.

"There is only one reason why I would consider this action. Despite this one disaster, I feel you show a great deal of promise. There would, however, be conditions. Firstly, you will not continue French at high school, and secondly, that you make every effort to justify my faith in you."

I simply said, "Thank you, sir. I will try to justify your belief in me."

What a teacher! What kid could not be affected by such a situation? Certainly, it made an indelible impression on me. To this day, I have never forgotten that experience. Contrary to a perfect ending to this incident, it did not magically make me into a thoroughly conscientious student, who gained the straight A's, of which I was capable, but I did make sure that I gained the results that would ensure my future ambitions, and aimed for excellence in my areas of enthusiasm.

How did this year affect my teaching philosophy?

Not noticeably at the time, of course, but it had important implications later. My improved performance due to being given responsibility for the first time, taught me the value of children feeling that they were contributing in some way. To be given a responsibility, no matter how large or how small, improves pride in self, an attitude so vital in developing overall performance. Responsibility must, of course, be earned, or it has far less worth, but the carrot should be offered, and the child encouraged to accept it. A teacher should be ready with gentle prompts and advice on the carrying out of this responsibility, and to be observant and quick to praise when a child does it well, or at least to the best of his or her ability. That year also taught me the importance of every child feeling that he or she is capable of performing well in at least one activity, and have the achievement recognised. This greatly improves performance in all other areas of effort.

Miss Divine's knack of being so interested in what I had to say, and the way she smiled fondly when looking at me, also left a marked impression on me. Her quiet voice intrigued me. At last a teacher didn't shout, at me in particular, and at the class in general. I determined that I would not shout when I became a teacher. If I became angry, I would show that anger by lowering my voice, rather than making it louder. As teachers raise their voices, trying to be heard, the children automatically respond by becoming noisier, thus the teacher yells even louder to be heard over their noise. A very noisy classroom is not conducive to effective education.

Probably most pertinent to my philosophy was Mr. White's interest in the wellbeing of each, and every one of his pupils, even me. He clearly demonstrated this in his efforts to help me by taking such an extreme action to provide me with the chance to achieve my potential. It was obvious that he was vitally interested in the overall needs, and the future of the children he taught, not just in gaining satisfactory examination results. Furthermore, he was prepared to go the extra mile to attend to those needs. Like him, I would also spend time in the school-ground, enjoying the contact with the children.

It may seem very surprising that a child of that age, particularly one whose name many teachers regarded as a swear word, should be so committed to becoming a teacher himself, and to think about how he might perform the role. Strange as it seems, this was the case with me. I never veered from that determination, and even began, during that period of my life, to formulate a few of the thoughts on how I would do the job. The above ideals became implanted in my psyche, though not really consolidated until they were re-enforced at the age of sixteen, when I became a student teacher.

I learnt from Mr. White how important it was to know and love your pupils, and be prepared to spend extra time with them, to be innovative in your approach, and in no way tolerate bullying in your school. I did, in fact, learn far more from him, but that occurred some years later, when I began my student teacher role.

My three years at high school were rather uneventful for me, probably due to being banned from football and athletics due to the heel injury I had sustained the year before enrolling. The school boasted an elite reputation, regularly gaining the highest percentage of matriculation passes in the state. I learnt later, that it also produced the highest percentage of first year university dropouts at that time –This could possibly be explained by the fact that information was pounded into our brains, but we were not taught how to learn. For example, the school library was out of bounds for students – it was only for teacher use. The school taught me to hate Shakespeare, as we were forced to study and dissect 'The Merchant of Venice', without seeing a performance, or even performing it ourselves. How boring! I have no doubt that it remedied those faults in future years, as it continued to be highly respected.

Two teachers only, at that school, left an impression on me.

Stephen Whawell had retired at the age of sixty-five. He missed his teaching so much that he returned to the school at aged sixty-seven. He had taught my father in the country high school at Castlemaine thirty-five years before he met me. Close to four hundred new pupils were assembled in the main assembly hall to be allotted to eight form 3 classes. Old Stephen was the only teacher supervising this process. He called out a name, that boy stood and shouted, "Sir!", and was allotted to a room number. Eventually I heard my name.

"Donald Leigh Roberts," old Stephen called.

"Sir!" I shouted, standing near the centre of the hall.

He glared over the top of his glasses. After a few moments he slowly stated,

"Donald Leigh Roberts, brother of Kenneth Earle, nephew of Leigh Roberts, Castlemaine, son of Ernest Earle Roberts, Castlemaine."

"Correct Sir," I confirmed.

After studying me for a few moments, he stated slowly and deliberately,

"Hm. I will be keeping my eye on you. Room 8D."

I would not forget old Stephen, and would emulate some of his tricks with chalk, and use some of his witty comments.

After three years at high school, Dad explained without much enthusiasm, that he would support me in my final year if I really wanted to complete it. If you intended to be a secondary teacher, you had to do your matriculation or year twelve. This was optional, but unnecessary for primary teaching. My enthusiasm to attend year 12 was even less than my father's, thus, at the tender age of 16 years and 4 months, I left school.

Because of what followed it proved to be one of the best decisions of my life.

****

Chapter 2

TEACHER TRAINING

Before beginning my term of student teaching I enjoyed a few other experiences that helped prepare me.

At the age of 12, I attended a Methodist Boys' Camp at Ocean Grove. As I was appointed to be one of the group leaders, I had several responsibilities, on which I thrived. Being a competitive beast myself, I revelled in all the inter-group competitions, which varied from tent and surroundings care and waiting on tables and kitchen duties, through sporting activities, to preparing and presenting concert items. I was also made captain of one of the two cricket teams that competed against each other, and against a team consisting of the camp leaders. I enjoyed this role, and learned many lessons on leadership through trial and error, and through the guidance provided to us by camp leaders.

Throughout the ensuing years, I remembered all this, and at the age of 15, decided to become a junior camp leader at that year's camp at Ocean Grove. This experience taught me much about handling a group of boys, their needs and the types of mischief many of them planned, most of which I had tried myself in the past. There wasn't much they could put over me.

One incident perhaps rates a mention. Due to the regular occurrence of dangerous rips during the mornings, swimming in the ocean beach during that time slot was banned.

It was my responsibility to supervise a game of beach cricket one morning. Three boys went a few minutes ahead with the equipment to set up a pitch. As can happen, the temptation of a swim became too much for one lad to resist.

By the time I arrived he had already been swept out to sea by a rip. I had no choice but to attempt to save him – he was my responsibility. After what seemed like hours, I lay utterly exhausted on the beach, with the lad safe beside me. Lacking knowledge concerning rips, I had fought that rip with almost fatal consequences. What I didn't know, but should have been told, was that I should have allowed the rip to carry me out, then swum sideways until I was clear of the rip, before swimming towards the shore. My superiors were most remiss to allot me that responsibility so ill-informed.

As well as learning this, be it too late, I learned the importance of knowing all possible safety measures, particularly concerning physical activities, when supervising children, and picked up many tips on organizing a group of children and gaining their co-operation.

Also at the age of fifteen, I became very aware of something lacking at my church. There were many activities available to we teenagers, and a mid-week function was organised for young girls, but nothing was done to involve lads between eight and twelve years old. I felt this void should be filled and planned to do something about it. Firstly, I attended a National Fitness weekend leadership course. After gaining enthusiastic response to be part of my planned program from a mate a couple of years older than me, I approached the church leaders for their approval.

Church leaders always seem very keen on supporting enthusiasm, but are less inclined to support the funding of that enthusiasm. If I were to run a successful boys' club, some basic equipment would be of great advantage. When I, as a last resort, suggested that I would make such things as a multi-level vaulting box, a beat board and a balance board, and organise some girls to sew beanbags, they agreed to provide the necessary materials. As well, I managed to scrounge a cast-off tumbling mat, boxing gloves and a variety of balls from a gymnasium. The club proved to be very popular, and I learnt a great deal about handling a group of boys. Their enthusiasm and obvious enjoyment made it very worthwhile. My fellow leader was a lovely bloke, the oldest son of a large family and substitute-father to his younger siblings – I could not have chosen a better co-leader. However, he had one fault – he was a plumber with no conception of his enormous strength. He suggested he and I give the boys a start in the boxing program by fighting a demonstration bout of a round or two. I was a competent boxer, having won an under 11 tournament at the age of nine, but he was a couple of years older and possessed that incredible strength found in very few men. During our exhibition bout, he proceeded to batter me almost into oblivion. Taking advantage of a short lull, I managed to gasp out a plea for mercy.

"Cammy, we are trying to teach the boys the noble art of self-defence, not how to murder someone."

Of course, he was most apologetic.

One other activity taught me another aspect of instructing – this time with girls. On Saturday mornings, I coached a girls' netball team for a season.

As you have no doubt now realised, I had considerable experience in dealing with children before I began my teacher training, which gave me a distinct advantage over many of my fellow-students. Furthermore, some of us, who had not reached the minimum teachers' college entry age of seventeen, took advantage of the student teacher scheme, the last time ever that it was offered. This was probably about the best decision we ever made, providing us with the best possible early training.

The course lasted for six months, placing us in a city primary school for two and a half days a week, and attending student teacher classes for the remainder of the week. The lectures were very informative, but the placement in the school was invaluable. The next few pages will clearly illustrate why.

I was placed at the same school I had attended myself, and from which I had left a mere three years earlier. This had the considerable advantage of convenience, as I could walk to school. However, the disadvantages far outnumbered the advantages, as many of the school children attending senior classes remembered me quite clearly. During my final year, I had been successful at sport and a house captain, both reasons to be well remembered. The children from my street, who attended the school, knew me well, as for years I had been the leader of the Westbrook Street Gang. This probably conjures up the vision of a rather violent child, but the worst activities of the gang were pinecone wars with the Hartwood St. Gang, with whom we were quite pally, except during our organised wars.

Teaching my own little sister in grade 3, was another considerable challenge.

As my sports-master, who was fond of me as a child, later informed me, my name, along with that of my best mate, had been regarded as a teacher swear word when I had attended the school. This meant he was very much in the minority of teachers who could tolerate me – and in fact, it made him probably stand almost alone in liking me. Fortunately for me, though, almost all those disapproving teachers had moved on to other schools during my three years away from the school, so I started with a reasonably clean reputation.

My memorable first day finally arrived. When I opened our front gate, it was to find all the children from the street waiting to walk with me to the school. I felt rather like the Pied Piper. With much fun and excitement, we finally arrived at the school gate, where they delighted in changing from calling me by my Christian name, to preceding my name with a Mr, spoken with mock respect.

Eventually I escaped from my escort to what I felt would be the relative peace of the senior school corridor. Wrong! Several older children surrounded me with enthusiastic pretend-respect. The outstanding boy, clear favourite to be head prefect and captain of all sporting teams, a lad whom I remembered well, and vice versa, bent low with a deep mocking bow uttering a rather disrespectful, "Mr Don, Sir!" Deep into the bow, he failed to notice the silent approach of Mr White. His doubled over backside abruptly came into violent contact with Mr White's boot, sending him flying forward in a most ungainly manner, onto his hands and knees.

"John," said Mr White, in a mild, matter-of-fact tone, as the said John attempted rather unsuccessfully to regain his composure, "I'd like you to meet *Mr* Roberts, our new teacher, who will be in charge of all sport this year. He will coach and select all school representative teams and appoint their captains. I doubt very much if he will be interested in anyone who doesn't show him his due respect."

After a short pause to allow all this to sink in, he added, "Perhaps, John, you would like to give Mr Roberts a welcome on behalf of the children."

To give the lad his due credit, he was equal to the occasion. Gathering himself together, he said, very formally,

"On behalf of the all the children, I would like to welcome you to the school, Mr Roberts. I am sure we will all enjoy you coaching us in our sport."

"Thank you, John. I look forward to it" I answered, in an equally formal manner.

Mr. White added, "Now, if you children would like to move outside, Mr Roberts and I have important matters to discuss."

The crowd quickly disbursed, finally awarding me peace.

Maybe many modern educationists would not approve of Mr. White's methods, but they certainly worked. He paved the way for me beautifully, and I received nothing but respect and co-operation from that day onwards.

If the children had been surprised by his statement, that was nothing compared to its effect on me. I was stunned by this information.

"Mr White," I stumbled, "I have of course played a lot of sport, but am hardly competent to take over your role."

"Don, after many unbroken years as sports master, I badly need a rest. Believe me, I am confident that you are more than competent to take over from me. Besides, do you really think that I can let go altogether? In no way will I ever interfere with your organisation or decisions, but I will always remain available if you need any advice or if you need an assistant."

He was as good as his word, never interfering, but always ready to help, advise and answer my questions. I learnt much wisdom from him, and, as was my way, I soaked it all in.

The afore-mentioned natural leader, John, rated my special attention. In every classroom and in the larger school community, you will find natural leaders, not many, but they are extremely important to the attitudes of the school. The whole senior grade, also strongly influences the rest of the school population, either for good or for bad. Thus, it is most important that teachers make the extra effort to develop a responsible and reliable grade six. The same principle applies to individual leaders.

It was as early as when I was in grade 3, playing cricket in the schoolyard nets, that the seed of this theory was sown. Being the smallest participant by far, I was forced to field close in at slips, the most unpopular and dangerous position, as there was little space between the batsman and the surrounding cyclone wire netting. It was the only way I could gain possession of the ball, thus being able to have a bowl. To manage to have a bat, one had to either bowl a batsman out or take a catch.

On one occasion the school head prefect, who was also captain of the school cricket team and opening fast bowler, bowled one of his thunderbolts. It was snicked straight at me in slips, and disappeared. Only I knew what had happened to it. My mother made all our clothes. When sewing our short pants, she made a flap instead of a zip, for use when the need arose to relieve pressure. Freakishly the ball had gone straight through this small hole and lodged in my groin, miraculously causing no damage or even discomfort. Gleefully I thrust my hand through that same hole, clasped the cricket ball, pulled it out and held it high, screeching that glorious, time honoured shout, "Howzat!!"

"Not out!" shouted the batsman. "Donny didn't catch it. It caught itself."

Of course, the final decision was left to he who must be obeyed, due to his lofty office as the school cricket captain and head prefect. After suitable consideration, he imperiously raised his finger and decreed the batsman to be out.

"It hasn't touched the ground and Donny has got hold of it. That makes it a catch." Thus, was an argument, and possibly even a scuffle, averted by the presence and action of a respected pupil leader.

This didn't seem too significant at the time, but the memory of it returned to me in my student teaching days, when I was developing my teaching theories. I always concentrated early on developing these leaders and senior grade standards, and it proved to be of great value in gaining the desired school attitudes.

My organised education in this, my chosen vocation, began in the principal's office. During the first fortnight, I experienced the organisation of a school from its hub, while performing the duties of messenger boy, taking instructions to teachers, and supplies such as art paper, coloured paper squares, blackboard necessities like chalk, dusters, and large rulers to classrooms. Boxes and parcels of supplies were delivered to the office and either distributed directly to classrooms, or found homes in the storeroom. The phone ran hot with official calls and calls from parents. Many of the latter called at the office, and misplaced and new children had to be found classroom homes. All seemed like organised chaos with so many things happening at once. Principals, or Head Teachers, as we called them then, do desperately need secretaries.

After the first fortnight, I had two main roles. My sporting responsibilities began, and with ever-available advice from Mr White, I put much thought and planning into it. Some recess and lunch times

I was obliged to spend in the staffroom, so the teachers and I could get to know and help each other, but I spent as much time as possible in the school ground playing with, and becoming well acquainted with the children. At the same time, I was assessing talent, both playing and leadership, storing up knowledge for my approaching role of selection and training of teams to represent the school. I revelled in this role and loved every minute of it.

Two great benefits came out of this period of time. Firstly, I developed a comfortable rapport with the children, before long knowing more children and more about them than any of the long-serving teachers. Secondly, I was storing up the knowledge concerning their abilities and needs. I thoroughly enjoyed these informal times with the children.

My second responsibility was spending time in every classroom, learning the techniques for teaching all the age groups. The upper grades presented me with few problems, but there was much to learn about the younger children. Each teacher had his or her own individual style with both qualities and faults. Although I felt a bit presumptuous in making judgements, I became very perceptive, and soon learnt to assess what was working well and what didn't. Interestingly, I probably learnt quite as much, possibly even more, from the teachers' faults than from their successful efforts. Normally I hate negativity, but it soon led to positivity, as I planned what I would do instead. Of particular interest to me, was keeping every child busy and interested, as my past problem misbehaviour, I realised, had certainly stemmed to some degree from lack of challenge. This appeared to me to be the weakest point of the program – teachers often failed to address this need and appeared to be quite disinterested in doing much about it. All children were given the same work, whatever their ability – some faltered, it suited some, and others were quickly finished, looking for something to do. I wasn't sure of the solution, but it was something to which I would give much thought.

Before long, filling the role of the replacement teacher when teachers were absent was added to my activities. I well remember my eight-year-old sister's embarrassment when I had to take over her class for a week.

"What should I call you?" she gasped.

I assured her she could use any name that made her feel comfortable, even 'Don', as I was still her brother, and everyone knew that. She finished up avoiding calling me by any title.

Teacher training in those days consisted of two years in teachers' college, but if you wished to gain promotion past the lower levels you had to complete two-week vacation schools in various subject areas and follow them up with a year of practical classroom teaching of these subjects. Only a few of us were able to benefit from the about to be discarded student teaching period before college. I am so grateful for having had that chance. That six months was of great benefit to me and gave me an enormous advantage over my fellow students, who had gone straight from secondary school to teachers' college. This advantage was most obvious on teaching rounds at schools. I could walk through the school gate and chat naturally with the children, whereas many of my fellow teacher students, would feel awkward and embarrassed, and hope to avoid children on their way into the safety of the school building. Also, the information that lecturers tried to teach us made immediate sense to me.

I remain still, an advocate for that type of practical training.

So, you see that I had much experience before entering teachers' college, beginning with my school days at a large school and the tiny one teacher rural school, through my work in camps and as a leader of a club, to coaching and student teaching. All contributed something towards the philosophy of teaching that I was developing, as did experiences for years to come.

Many of the following I became aware of during my years of schooling, but of course I didn't really formulate them until my student teacher experience.

Basically, the philosophy I developed before I started my formal teachers' college training was as follows :-

1. Like the children and demonstrate this affection openly – they will respond in like manner.
2. Be friendly, but firm – if a child does step out of line, pull him or her up immediately.
3. Be consistent with children – what is expected behaviour, should be expected at all times.
4. Be yourself and act naturally – children immediately see right through a teacher who tries to appear to be someone he is not.
5. Retain your sense of humour, and be ready to employ it often. Laugh – if something appeals to you as amusing, enjoy it fully,

whether in front of the children or not. They love a teacher who laughs, particularly if the joke happens to be on the teacher himself. Never laugh at anything that happens to a child if there is a remote chance that it will embarrass him or her.

6. Make school life for your children both interesting and fun – a bored child is a problem child (I know, as that described me in my school days). Number facts and tables must be learnt, but are best learnt through games and competitions. Essays should be on topics which are of great interest to the children, and should be introduced in a manner that makes them keen to begin writing. Acting a situation, going on an excursion within or away from the school, pictures or a film, class discussions, doing an illustration, are all helpful tools to employ. If a child wants to write, that writing will be his or her best. I believed this theory then, and proved it with personal experience later. At school, I always passed English Expression, but never excelled at it. It never inspired me to put in much effort. When I left home and was teaching in the remote farming community, I wanted my city family to really appreciate what I was experiencing. To achieve this, I put much time and effort into writing long and detailed letters home, describing my environment, my experiences, the people with whom I became involved, and my feelings. My mother kept them for the rest of her life. Looking through her belongings many years later, I found and read them, most surprised to find how well they had been written, especially as the author had been a very average English student such a short time before writing them.

7. Singing, acting, and playing are all activities that children love. Give them the chance to enjoy these as often as possible and encourage all children to participate.

8. Aim to develop the whole child, to enrich all children's personality and character, and broaden their experience, not just pump knowledge into young minds.

9. Children need self-confidence. Every child, even the least academically blessed, must feel that he or she is good at something, even if it is at art, craft, sport, singing or perhaps just being a reliable monitor. Provide every child with the chance to succeed, and be generous with praise when it is deserved.

10. Challenge children – they should need to strive to succeed. At the same time, be sure not to ruin self-confidence. Always begin with the simple, then move gradually to the more challenging.

11. Go outside and play with them whenever possible. The best way to develop a rapport with children is to join in their play.

12. Always be on the lookout for the slightest sign of bullying and nip it in the bud. All children deserve to be happy at school. Playing in the school-ground with the children is most helpful in detecting bullying early, and in eliminating, even preventing it occurring.

13. Whenever possible and educational, take the children out of the school environment. Only one teacher at my training school did so. Fortunately, I accompanied her and her class, where I delighted in their enjoyment and observed the benefits.

14. Children learn by absorbing information through the senses, remembering that information, and finding out how to apply it to situations. I had a theory that the memory needed extra attention. Many children were a bit scatty, their minds quickly flitting off to other thoughts, so I devised several simple memory training activities and competitions. Sometimes I would write on the board, sometimes just tell them, sometimes allow them to write, something like a number, a phone number, perhaps two or three objects. This would happen first thing in the morning. If they could remember and repeat it later in the day, or at the end of the day, they could score points for their house or be rewarded in some other way. Gradually I would increase the time between being given the information and recalling it, until they had to remember for a week or more. Complexity of the information to be remembered would also gradually increase. The improvement in memory was quite extra-ordinary and they loved the activities.

All this I had in my head before I went to teachers' college for my formal training. What was left to learn? Actually, there was much still to learn, and all my theories had to be consolidated and revised, with some changes and additions. But compare this with some of my peers who went straight to college from attending school themselves, with no planning or previous thought, and often with no experience whatsoever with younger children. It is rather obvious that I had an enormous head start over them. In fact, if for some reason, I could not have attended teachers' college, I feel I would have been reasonably well equipped to begin a teaching career.

I still strongly feel that this form of apprenticeship learning, holds a considerable advantage over the theory first approach of attending university straight from school.

Of course, my two years in teachers' college did much to consolidate my ideas, modify them, and expand my personal development. So, what did I gain from those two years at a teacher training college?

Firstly, I matured considerably. That does in no way mean that I left my wild youth behind. On the contrary, I was most fortunate that some of my more foolish escapades did not cause me to be expelled. One can even learn from these.

One naughty act doesn't mean a bad child. Everyone deserves a second and perhaps even more chances. Mr White gave me a second chance at the age of twelve, because he had faith in me. So too, did the senior psychology lecturer at teachers' college. He watched as I dropped ten feet from a window, followed by my partner in crime, down onto the gymnasium roof, raced across the gym roof, and leapt to freedom - all this to escape a very boring lecture. He could have had us expelled. We knew that he saw us, and he knew that we knew he saw us. Instead of the expulsion, however, for three weeks he appeared outside our lecture rooms as we exited, without saying a word, while giving us the evil eye until we were out of sight – sheer psychological torture. He then left for an extended overseas conference, still not saying a word to us, but obviously, to our extreme relief, giving us a second chance. He proved to be a good judge of character as we both had successful teaching careers.

When I say that I matured, I refer to gaining through many experiences, the ability to handle a variety of situations. I learnt to work as part of a team, to talk with people in authority without being overawed, and to feel comfortable with people from a number of different walks of life. Through teaching rounds in various districts, I experienced handling children from different backgrounds, from the disadvantaged to the privileged, children of wide ranging abilities, and from different ethnic origins.

Teachers' college also extended and revised my subject knowledge, which was necessary, and suggested methods of instruction in all areas.

The majority of this teaching skill, I agreed with and absorbed, though I retained the right to use my own methods in some fields where my opinions differed.

****

Chapter 3

MY TEACHING CAREER BEGINS.

As the college training neared its end, we students could not wait to go out and put our training into practice in the big wide world. Very few of us would gain a permanent position immediately, so could be sent anywhere there was a need, at any time.

I was both lucky and unlucky. My letter sent me to a school only a mile from home, which was most convenient, but, of course, did not fulfil my long-held dream of teaching in a farming district. Never mind, there were many more years ahead for that.

Never count your chickens before they are hatched. Due to start on Monday July 3rd 1953, I received a letter on the preceding Friday, which said, 'Change of plans – you will take up a position at Mildura Central School on Monday morning.' That was 365 miles away. There was no time to waste. With a sense of excitement and anticipation, I quickly packed, and boarded the *Vinelander*, the overnight train to Mildura, at 9.30 that very night. Welcomed by my head teacher, whom I had contacted before I left, I was informed that I would be living in a guest house half a mile from the school, and would be teaching a Grade 4 of forty-eight children plus an extra ten children of widely varying ages, with learning difficulties. Apparently, due to the loss of a member of staff, the opportunity grade, which was a special grade for children with learning problems found in most larger schools, had to be split up. Why I was given ten of them I'm not sure, as I now had fifty-eight children in a smaller than average sized classroom. Desks were pressed up against three walls, with several more on the teacher's platform in front of the blackboard, and still I could just manage to sidle along aisles between desks. It would be hard to imagine a more challenging task for an eighteen-year-old, just out of Teachers' College.

Never mind, at eighteen years of age you are bulletproof. Difficulties are just there to overcome. How could my philosophy of teaching help me in this situation? Probably, by remaining positive and cheerful and gaining the affection and cooperation of the children would be a good start, and would contribute to overcoming the physical discomfort. I decided also to be flexible and innovative. The winter weather in Mildura was consistently mild and sunny, so I scrounged a portable blackboard and took the children outside under a wide-spreading shady tree for as many lessons as possible. Arranging the program to be full of interest, with plenty of physical activities, singing, and acting, also helped.

After three months, I was delighted with the manner in which things were proceeding. The children were achieving well, I was enjoying my accommodation, regularly played sport, and helped train a square-dance set to compete in the Australian Championships. This wonderful social life included a beautiful and vivacious girlfriend.

Then the bombshell dropped.

"You begin teaching at a one-teacher school tomorrow morning."

My head teacher delivered this startling news on the first Sunday in October.

"Where on earth is this place?" I asked.

"I don't know," he said apologetically. "I couldn't find it on my road map. But the children there are apparently totally out of control and have taken over from their teacher, so you have to replace him tomorrow."

We young teachers had to expect anything, but this was at first a bit of a shock. He contacted me an hour later, saying, "Change of plans. You are still going, but not until Thursday. The teacher who had to leave there is swapping positions with you. Before you leave you must settle him in here."

He arrived on Monday morning. To my surprise, he was 23 years old and 6 feet 3 inches tall. What were these children – monsters? Just turned nineteen, I was 5 feet 7 inches tall, and nine and a half stone wringing wet. Probably, I should have been shaking in my shoes. I wasn't. This man, despite his imposing physical appearance, spoke without any expression and exuded no energy. His body language was all wrong for inspiring children. After the initial shock and thinking about the enjoyable set-up I was leaving behind, particularly my girlfriend, I even began to look forward to the challenge ahead. After all, my dream of teaching and living in a farming district was about to be fulfilled – the whole set-up began to excite me. Obviously, I would be tested – these 32 children in grades prep to year nine had taken over the school, and decided what they would and would not do. That, apparently didn't include any form of schoolwork. This attitude would have to be reversed, but strangely it never entered my mind that I might fail to do this. I had yet to meet children from whom I could not gain co-operation. It seemed to me that I would just have to set new standards and be consistent in demanding them. Even so, I did not kid myself – it would not be easy, but I believed it would be achievable.

At 9.30 p.m. on Wednesday, I boarded the 'Vinelander' again. Eventually, I had discovered that the school was situated in the North-west Mallee district of Victoria. The district was sometimes referred to as 'The Gateway to the Outback'. This was certainly country territory. Seventy miles south of Mildura I would leave the Vinelander at Ouyen, and wait until 5.30 am to board the tiny diesel one-carriage train bound for my new home.

Having boarded the Vinelander train at Mildura, heading for what promised to be an amazing experience, my mind buzzed with plans, so it seemed little time before I reached Ouyen. Within seconds of disembarking at the Ouyen Station at about 11pm, I found myself alone on the station platform, freezing, despite it being early October – there would be a heavy frost come morning.

This would not do. I headed for nearby bushland and soon returned with an armful of dead branches. It took all the station toilet paper to start the fire in the waiting room, but it was soon blazing cheerily. Life felt good again.

After boarding the Diesel, which I quickly nicknamed 'The Rattler,' at 5am, we rattled west in the dark. Before long the sun crept over the horizon and gradually a panorama of rolling green plains unfolded before my delighted eyes. This green grassland was punctuated by clumps of low, multi-trunked eucalypts, which I soon learnt were the Mallee gums, from which the Mallee roots we had burned in our Melbourne fireplaces originated.

To one who had expected sandy desert country, it was quite a surprise. Of course, my first views of it were at the time of the year when it looked its best.

As the train pulled in to at a small railway siding, I realised that I had arrived.

****

CHAPTER 4

SECOND TOUGH INITIATION

Lugging my large case and the two boxes of teaching aids I had made or collected, under my arms, I stepped off the train to be confronted by a middle-aged lady.

"Are you the new 'teach'?" she asked.

"Yes," I just got this answer out before she again attacked.

"Do you play football?"

"Yes."

"Do you play tennis?"

"Yes."

"You don't square dance too, do you?"

"Yes."

"Oh Good! That last bloke was dead wood. Come and have some breakfast."

So, these were the requirements of being a satisfactory country teacher. Obviously, I had passed the test as a teacher – no question about teaching itself. I did wonder if I would have eaten breakfast that morning if my answers had been 'no'.

After a sumptuous cooked breakfast, I wandered off up the winding dirt track that led to the school about four hundred yards away. Only the occasional rustling of lizards and birdcalls disturbed the peace and almost total silence. I loved it.

The bushland view was suddenly changed by my first glimpse of the green roof of the tiny one-roomed school appearing through the leaves ahead.

Something else also soon appeared – something that looked distinctly like ending the peace.

A thirteen-year-old boy filled the gateway, chewing a blade of long dry grass and glaring balefully in my direction. This looked like being a far more difficult welcome to handle than the lady on the station platform.

"Probably the leader of the pack," I thought. "Win this one, Don, or reboard the departing train tonight."

Since learning of my fate, I had spent some time in planning my tactics. I would still employ my friendly but firm policy, but first I would need to establish my authority. Now was the time.

Without slowing, in fact instead quickening my pace slightly, I headed for him. He showed no sign of giving way.

"I'm going through that gate, son and it seems you are in my way." I guess that wasn't the smartest of tactics, but it was my instinctive reaction.

I maintained the pace of my approach.

At the last minute, he jumped aside with a sudden grin. "Well, so I was, Sir."

Continuing my approach to the school, I was followed closely by my new shadow, whose name I discovered was Jamie.

Reaching the front door, I opened it with the large key and entered. I had not expected total cleanliness and an orderly appearance, but what confronted me brought out an involuntary gasp. The teacher's table was piled high, desks were in disarray, one tipped on its side, books, pens, pencils and rulers littered the floor, and the blackboard had what was obviously child scribble all over it.

"How do you work in a place like this?" I involuntarily gasped

His quick rejoinder of, "Oh! We don't work, Sir. We just muck about," was obviously a challenge.

I fixed his gaze to mine.

"Make that, 'We used to just muck about, Jamie.' There are going to be some big changes around here. Mucking about is out."

He attempted to, but failed to stare me down. Suddenly, accepting the change, he turned, hung his bag on a hook, and said, "What would you like me to do to help, sir?"

Working diligently together, we had almost restored order when the grating of gears signalled the arrival of the old Bedford, red and cream school bus.

I went out to meet the horde as it tumbled out of the bus. Wary eyes on me, they raced over to Jamie with a stage-whispered, "What's he like, Jamie?"

I didn't hear his answer, as old Dougie, the farmer who owned and drove the school bus, demanded my attention by sitting on the step of the bus, rolling a cigarette, and handing me the makings. I hunkered down, bushman style and we shared a chat as we smoked.

"You'll have to stand on them or they'll run all over you," he said in a mournful tone, shaking his head. He made my mind flash to Father John O'Brien's character, Hanrahan. I almost expected him to add, "Or we'll all be rooned."

"I'll stand on them, and stand hard if necessary," I assured him, using his wording.

It did become necessary at lunchtime, when little David in Grade 4, defied my instruction to pick up the lunch scraps he had tossed away.

"Don't hafta if I don't want to," was his rather insolent response.

There was no way I would accept defiance or direct disobedience, so I strapped him lightly on the hand and he obeyed.

That night I heard, and was meant to hear,

"Ha! Ha! It didn't hurt!" come floating through the air from the departing bus.

It did hurt the following morning at assembly, in front of all the other children.

The strap then went into the drawer, and almost never needed to come out again.

However, my task was definitely not over. These children had not applied themselves to work for nearly twelve months and had forgotten how it was done.

At the end of day two, Julie, in Grade 6 let out a huge sigh. "I'm worn out working," she said in an exhausted tone.

"Actually, I'm a little disappointed," I said, shaking my head. "I like to finish the day with some sport, and today we can't, because you didn't finish the work in time."

Old Dougie had told me they really loved their sport. Their ears pricked up – the challenge was offered and accepted. From that day on, we rarely finished the day with less than half an hour of sport, with all work completed first.

When I gave them the chance to sing and act, they excelled and loved it, so these activities became an integral part of our program. This led to putting on an exciting end-of-year concert, consisting of a gymnastic display, followed by several skits and songs on stage, and culminating with a nativity scene. As there was no electricity to light the concert, I had to construct lighting from borrowed Tilley kerosene pressure lamps, and shades that I constructed from corrugated iron to direct the light. Santa Claus was expected to call in after the concert. While we awaited him, I conducted some games. At last the children heard a shout.

"He's coming!"

My games and I were forgotten and I was almost knocked down in the rush for the door. Alas, false alarm. This and other false alarms to follow caused much disappointment.

Eventually he did arrive, but quite late. Apparently, he had almost reached the hall when he dropped something. Bending over he ripped the entire seam of his red trousers open, and had to return to his general store for Mrs Claus to conduct repairs.

Fortunately, I developed a wonderful rapport with the children, and am still in close touch with several of them, sixty years later.

To inform you on how I developed this relationship, perhaps I can describe some situations.

Soon after my arrival the children asked for a bird walk. This created a slight problem. I knew sparrows, magpies, blackbirds, hawks and crows. I recognised when a bird was part of the parrot family, but that was about it. I stalled.

"Leave it with me," I suggested. "I'll plan something."

"You don't need to do that, sir. Jamie can take us."

I looked at Jamie and received a confident nod.

"Now seems a good time, then," I said. "Let's go."

Our guide amazed me. His knowledge was extraordinary and never found wanting. He located and explained the habits of numerous birds. Finally, he shouted,

"Look! Frogmouth Owl!"

"Yeah! Yeah!" shouted his disciples.

I looked and looked, but could see nothing.

Noticing my dilemma, Jamie showed great patience and understanding.

"See that stumpy thing on that horizontal branch across the track, Sir?"

"Of course I do," I said.

"Keep watching it, Sir."

I watched seeing no change. He then lobbed a small stick next to it. One eye opened then closed again.

"I saw its eye!" I shouted, genuinely excited.

"Good on 'yer', Sir." said Jamie.

"Good on 'yer', Sir!" shouted his disciples.

At last I was first to see a bird.

"Look, pigeon!" I shouted, frightening it and causing it to fly off.

"Yes sir," sighed Jamie, patronisingly. "It was a bronze-wing. I was waiting to get closer, so I could point out the difference between it and the topknot. Topknots are wonderful eating, sir, but are protected, so you can only shoot what you need for your meal." I had been put nicely in my place.

Sighing, I swallowed my pride and we continued, all having a wonderful and educational day.

My nervousness of snakes was well documented. One morning, I had enjoyed the walk through bushland to school, as usual. As I approached the school I noticed a head with a face alight with anticipation, being rapidly withdrawn behind a far corner of the school building.

It started alarm bells. Some mischief was afoot – I was warned and prepared. Passing the school tank, I suddenly saw the head of a snake protruding from the corner of the entrance cement slab. This was too much of a co-incidence.

Snake? No Problem.

With a wild yell, I fearlessly, even heroically, charged the snake, giving that poisonous head a vicious kick. Continuing casually on to the door, I pretended not to notice the head with the unbelieving, stunned expression, peering around the second tank. As I placed the key in the lock, I casually instructed that head, "Get rid of that snake I have just killed please, Jamie."

"Aw! You knew Sir, didn't you," he disappointedly complained.

I had started at the school on October 10th 1953, and at the start of the following year I went to board at Jenkins' farm. The family consisted of old Dougie Jenkins, a slow talking, easy going friendly farmer, Mum Jenkins, mother to all, 17-year-old Helen, who had just left a secondary boarding school, 14-year-old irrepressible Joan, who attended that boarding school, but was home for a couple more weeks before her school year started, young Doug in Grade 6, Jane in Grade 4, and Trevor, the farm hand. They quickly became my family, welcoming me from the start.

Would there be a problem? How could I be a family member, open to pranks like walking around a corner into a brown paper bag water bomb, and at the same time, be a respected teacher? It never proved to be a problem. I just said to the children, "I am two people, a fun family member at home, and a teacher from whom you receive no privileges that are not available to every other child the moment we enter school, or when the first kid boards the bus if I am driving. They never once crossed that line and remain my friends to this day.

The pride and joy of my life was my 1918 Riley tourer. Being of that vintage, it did have a few problems. One of these was that it had a large open flywheel, which had several worn ring gears. To give the starter a chance to work, I carried in the back seat a steel rod, with which I would push the flywheel around until the starter could engage a healthy ring gear. In the middle of performing this operation one recess time, I felt my elbow grabbed and tugged a bit as 8-year-old John, son of a rally driving and engineering freak, swung himself up onto the mudguard.

"'Watcha doin, Sir?" he asked.

"Turning the flywheel to find a ring gear that's not too worn, so the starter engages, John," I explained.

"Fair enough," he commented with obvious understanding, as he gazed into the simple, in fact, rather primitive workings under the bonnet.

"Where's the air cleaner?" he said, after a short examination.

"It doesn't have one, John" He shook his head in amazement.

"Where's the distributor?" came next.

"Doesn't have one of them either, John." I was about to explain that it had a magneto instead, but he interrupted me.

Scratching his head in puzzlement, he said, slowly and emphatically, "How the bloody hell does it go, Sir?"

Carefully not noticing the language, I responded with, "I don't really know, John. It's amazing, isn't it."

"Sure is, Sir." Having satisfied his curiosity, I was obliged to flex my arm, as he again grabbed my elbow and swung himself back down from the car, and raced off to his next absorbing moment.

John's young brother, Bill, and a lass named May, began their school life on the same day. What a contrast! May cried pitifully for the first hour, while Bill wandered around, hands in pockets, casing the joint.

I let all the children play outside for an extra hour before starting, to allow the wonderful senior girls to comfort May and settle her in, which they did with great kindness and understanding.

This, however, did not suit Bill at all. Arriving through the doorway, hands deep in pockets, he asked,

"Where are I 'gunna' sit?"

I showed him to his seat.

"Is that OK, Bill?" I asked.

"Yeah! When are we 'gunna' start work?" he demanded in a most dissatisfied tone."

Although I took the time to explain about May and her troubles, it was clearly obvious that he was only slightly appeased.

A short time later, I felt an urgent tug on my trousers, and shortly after that the same tug again.

"When are we 'gunna' start work?" he impatiently demanded on both occasions.

"As soon as May settles down," I answered each time, suggesting he play with the other boys, who were thoroughly enjoying the delayed start.

When, very soon after, I felt that by now familiar tug, I forestalled him,

"We're 'gunna' start work now, Bill!"

"Good!" he shouted gleefully, scuttling off to be first in line.

It was usual to ease prep children into the school program employing play-way activities with toys, counting materials, and building blocks, reading of stories and drawing activities. This did not suit young Bill at all. He had come to school to do what he called 'proper work'. Soon he began to appear at older children's elbows, gazing at what they were doing.

On the second weekend, I happened to be where Bill's mum was. She came up to me and opened her mouth to speak. I forestalled her, as I had done to Bill, by saying,

"Bill's 'gunna' start proper work on Monday."

She smiled with relief and chuckled, "Thank goodness!" she sighed, then added, "been driving you crazy too, has he?"

"Let's say he can be rather persistent," I said, mimicking her chuckle.

That Monday morning, I met the arriving school bus as always, only to be greeted by Bill's head sticking well out of the window, obviously breaking the 'bums on seats' strict rule in his urgency.

"My mum says I'm 'gunna' start proper work this morning!" came floating ahead to me.

Who was I to argue? He started proper work that morning.

Brother number three, Ronny, started the following year.

"You think Bill is lively? Wait until you meet Ronny?" sighed Jenny in Grade 7, shaking her head.

She exaggerated not.

A few weeks after his arrival, I was seated on the thunder box (toilet), which was situated in scrubland well away from the school. It was lunchtime. Suddenly I felt something jab my bottom. My first thought was of a snake, but then I heard the flap at the back, drop into place, a stick tossed away, and the scuttling of feet. Snakes don't have feet.

Peaceful Performance Rudely Interrupted.

In my own good time, I exited through the door. There were twenty-eight worried pairs of eyes looking up at me. There should have been twenty-nine that day. The children of a one-teacher school become like your large family – one glance was enough to know who was missing.

"Ronny Davis!" I shouted.

A small red shirt rose from behind a log and 5-year-old Ronny shuffled towards me. I was having great difficulty holding back a helpless laugh, but I managed to glare at him. Slowly and with venom in my tone, I said,

"Ronny, if that ever happened again, I know one small boy whose bottom would be so sore he would not be able to sit down for a week."

Clearly, the message was understood, as he ruefully rubbed his bottom, and in deep thought answered,

"Yes, Sirrrr!"

Twenty-eight sighs of relief sounded. The expected crisis had been safely negotiated.

In this Mallee District it rarely rained, an average of only eleven inches a year. The children loved the rain.

One day it was absolutely pouring cats and dogs. All the children were standing inside the doorway admiring the downpour – that is, I thought they were all there. But, glancing out the window I saw Bill, hunkered down, wearing his sou'wester, happily sailing sticks down a fast-flowing rivulet. It looked great fun, but he would be getting soaked.

Going to the door amongst the children standing there, I bellowed, "Bill, come in out of that rain." Not a move, except to sail another stick.

He would have clearly heard. Most annoyed, I charged out into the heavy rain. As I was about to haul him up, his head turned upwards, and, with an angelic smile, he said,

"Tisn't Bill. It's Ronny."

This time I did burst into laughter, as I tucked him under my arm and carried him in out of the rain.

Soaked to the skin, I surveyed all the grinning faces. They explained to me that, as I was yelling his name, Bill was standing right next to me grinning and gazing up, but saying nothing – nor did any of them. They were lucky I loved them.

Little Lyn in Grade 1 came charging into the schoolroom, where I was correcting essays at the table. Pulling my knee out, she climbed onto it, reached up and pulled my face down to gain my undivided attention.

"It's running and they're running and it's running and they're running and you've 'gotta' come and see."

Finished delivering her most urgent message in such lucid (to her, anyway) fashion, she jumped down, grabbed my hand, and dragged me to the door, so I could go and see what I just had to see.

It was quite a sight. A goanna chase was in full flight – one poor goanna chased by more than twenty whooping hunters. Now and again the goanna would stop and turn. Knowing of a goanna's determination to climb anything vertical, as one, the hunters would throw themselves flat on their faces. When it took off again, they rose, all on cue, and continued the chase, much to Lyn's screeching delight.

Intrepid Hunters

Eventually, I took pity on the poor, badgered creature, blew my whistle and called the intrepid hunters back inside. Our afternoon program suddenly changed. This was too good to still follow the

41

planned day. We excitedly discussed all the habits of the fascinating goanna, then had an enthusiastic goanna running competition, which was so keenly and realistically contested that I had to declare them all winners. While they were hot, we wrote a story about George, the Gangly Goanna, which they then illustrated. The topic somehow developed into discussing the lizard family in general, and climaxed with a lizard search in the nearby bushland.

That poor maligned goanna had no idea what an educational treat it had instigated.

One day I was playing with a group of infants at morning recess when Jamie approached me.

"We go home now, Sir," he said.

"Well, I may permit that Jamie, but you would need to present a very strong case."

"I can do that, Sir. See that thin black line on the horizon?" He was pointing at the western horizon.

I saw it all right, but had no idea what it might be.

"I certainly do, Jamie. What on earth is it?"

"It's an approaching dust storm, Sir. They come up real fast, and can be pretty bad. I would reckon some cars and the bus will be here soon and they'll be in a hurry."

They were. Almost as he finished his prediction the first car skidded to a halt at the gate. The mother herded hers and her neighbour's children in after a brief greeting and accelerated off. As she left another car pulled up, followed shortly after by the school bus. It was quite a rushed, but organised exit.

"Do you want me to drop you off at Camm's, Don?" asked Doug. "It wouldn't be much fun here on your own."

"No, I'll stay here, Doug," I asserted. "From what I've heard Millie say about dust storms, there could be quite a clean-up needed after it."

"Suit yourself," said Doug, and left with a hurried wave.

What an extraordinary experience! As Jamie had warned, it *did* come fast and it *was* pretty bad. It did not sweep in or creep in – it rolled in like a tsunami wave. On its arrival, everything turned to an eerie dark brown. It seemed to block out everything - no sun at all could pierce its all-encompassing brown. In Melbourne, I had experienced what we regarded as severe dust storms, but I had never seen anything to remotely compare with this. Even with all doors and windows tightly shut, I had to tie a handkerchief around my head, covering my nose, to breathe. This situation lasted for one and a half hours, although it seemed much longer. Suddenly rain poured down and within minutes I went outside and breathed in deeply. The air smelled amazingly fresh, and was heavily scented by the many surrounding eucalypts.

Cleaning my school was a long, and should have been a tedious task, but I had great affection for that little schoolroom, so it proved to be a labour of love.

By the time I walked home down my favourite bush track, the rain had ceased, and the Mallee-gums had never looked or smelled better.

Millie had a far less rosy view of the world as she slaved to clean her house.

"Look at these cups!" she almost shrieked at me, showing the inch of dirt in cups that had been hanging in the kitchen dresser. I fear she had far less affection for her temporary fibro cement house than I had for my school.

A car passing through during the Christmas break had stopped for the occupants to have drink from one of our two tanks. Carelessly they had left the tap running – a thoughtless crime in that type of country. It was now dry and the other tank had developed a rust hole, and was also dry. I had been carting a large water bag to school for a few weeks, but I was keen to catch as much water as possible during the first rain. With this in mind, I had finally persuaded two farmers to come and help lift off and repair the holed tank. At 9.30 am I was sitting with my hat on the back of my head, a cigarette dangling from my mouth, busy soldering the hole in the base of the tank. As the men had arrived early I had not even opened the school. Without warning a shadow fell on me.

"Yes, mate, what can I do for you?" I said to the new arrival.

"For a start, you can open your school. Lessons should have begun half an hour ago."

What a time for the dreaded school inspector to arrive for his first inspection! He was not at all impressed with the initiative I had shown in performing the necessary repairs, continuing to find fault for most of the day. A composition lesson had gone over its scheduled time slot. The children were still writing on a topic that had enthused them. Officiously, he looked long and deliberately at his watch.

"Composition has gone overtime, Mr Roberts. It is vital in a one-teacher school to stick strictly to the time table."

By now I had taken enough from him.

"Educationally, it is important that children be allowed to finish something about which they are enthusiastically writing," I retorted. "I know where my priorities lie."

To his annoyance, the children were given the time to finish their stories, despite his obvious disapproval.

He stormed out of the room for a while, which disappointed me. I was primed for a fight. At lunch-time he walked around the school-ground and returned with a stumpy-tailed lizard in each hand. Triumphantly he held them out over my table, where I was busy filling out some forms he had demanded I complete, forms that I hadn't even previously known existed.

"You should be studying these with the children!" he boomed, obviously pleased with himself.

"If you go outside for ten minutes more, you'll probably find half a dozen more of them, as well as several other types of lizard and quite possibly a goanna, all of which we have studied in detail, and observed how they live in their natural environment," I informed him with considerable satisfaction.

Whether he squeezed a bit too hard in his annoyance, or whether the time of need had just arrived I know not, but one of his captives let go all over the work on my table.

"Oh! Charming chappie!" I snorted in disgust.

I did mean the lizard, but the way he stormed out again, perhaps he thought I meant him. I hoped so. The funny side of it all suddenly hit me, and I laughed heartily as he was leaving - again probably not wise in developing a relationship. His fault finding continued all afternoon, but at the end of the day, he was gracious enough to admit that his comments had all been in reference to about three per cent of my efforts. The other ninety-seven per cent was excellent, and if I stayed in his district it would be greatly to my future advantage. Hearing this after the wretched day he had put me through, I went very close to blotting my copybook again, but managed to hold back what I wished to say and was tempted to do.

What did this experience contribute to my philosophy? I decided that I would never teach according to the whims of authorities if I felt they were misinformed, or were polishing their own egos, as was sometimes the case. Such situations did arise in several later experiences with inspectors and some school principals. Always the best interests of my children would guide my decisions and actions. This attitude caused some confrontations with authority in the future as you will read. My approach on these occasions contrasted sharply with the majority of my fellow teachers, who regarded inspectors with awe, partly due to the authority an inspector held, and partly to further their own futures. My attitude did, in fact, affect the timing of my promotion on a couple of occasions.

Education in a one-teacher country school has many advantages. Children receive individual attention, they usually feel safe in their large family-type situation, they develop independence and initiative, and they learn to help others. The disadvantages are that they only experience one teacher, and they don't enjoy the chance to interchange and compete with a larger group of children of their age.

To counter these disadvantages, we teachers of the one-teacher schools organised an annual inter-school athletic sports meeting, and monthly group days with all schools attending the larger Underbool school. On these occasions, each teacher conducted programs of his particular specialty, for larger groups of similar age. Such activities as art, craft, dance, singing, drama, games, and gymnastics proved to be both popular, and of value to the children. As well as the group days, we conducted a couple of all-schools picnics.

It was at one of these picnics at the Pinnaroo Sports Ground, where I experienced my second dust storm. Doug, our farmer-cum-bus driver, was first to notice its approach. After he warned me, I gathered the children together, arranged for them all to use the toilets and loaded them into the bus for the obligatory head count. Little David Brown was missing. Quickly calming the mounting panic around me, I instructed the children to remain in the bus and arranged for old Doug to guard them. Seventeen-year-old Helen, his daughter and my part-time school sewing mistress, had come to help supervise. I instructed her to search the open areas and car parks, while I searched in the nearby bushland, where I felt sure he would be. Jamie wanted to help search, but, capable bushman though he was, I was not prepared to risk him, so I assured him that it was more important for him to be in charge of the smaller children. This he grudgingly accepted.

"Before long this storm could become frightening for a six-year-old," warned Helen.

Of that I was well aware.

"If you find him, have your father give two blasts on the bus's horn. I will do the same if I find him," I instructed her.

With great relief, shortly after our search began, I caught sight of him crouched down and gently poking a stumpy-tail lizard with a stick. I crouched down with him and watched for a few seconds.

"These stumpies really are sleepy, aren't they, Sir," he mused.

"They sure are," I agreed.

"I reckon their other name, 'sleepy lizards', is their best name," he added.

"Could be, David. Didn't you see the dust storm coming?" I asked.

"'Course I did, Sir," he assured me, sounding offended that I should doubt it. "I was coming back to the bus in a minute, but we're going to have to leave, so I just wanted to watch him a bit longer."

As so often happened I had to smile.

"Well, we must go right now, David. The bus is about to leave."

"Yeah, just like I reckoned. See ya, Stumpy," he regretfully sighed, as he rose to go with me.

Big sister, Marian, gave him the rounds of the table, told him what an idiot he was, and then spoiled her rebuke by giving him a hug of relief.

We headed off, unable to exceed ten miles an hour all the way home.

To successfully teach a one-teacher rural school it is necessary to prepare thoroughly and use capable older children as monitors, so that you can give your total attention to another group or individual child.

Soon after I arrived at the school I had appointed a very capable Grade 3 boy to hear the Grade 2 children read on the school steps. Not long after school had been dismissed, the monitor arrived back at school quite out of breath.

"She said I did and I didn't, and Mum said I had to come and tell you and you'd know the truth," he gasped between heaving breaths.

It was quite obvious that he hadn't done whatever it was she said he'd done, which eventually I discovered was telling the girl to lift her dress. It is easy to squeeze the truth out of a child who has lied. I quickly sorted it all out next morning.

All would have been well and the matter quickly forgotten, except that the girl's mother had rung everyone in the district, telling them what this dreadful boy had done to her daughter.

People were up in arms. The matter had to be resolved immediately. I called a meeting at the school the next night for all interested. All the parents and, in fact, everyone in the district, with the exception of the parents involved attended. I had previously sorted them out, and advised them not to attend.

At the meeting, I was confronted by a sea of angry faces.

Knees badly knocking, but fortunately hidden, I addressed the meeting, briefly explaining the facts of the situation, how I had solved the problem, and the stupidity of the community's reaction, which had made a mountain out of a molehill. I then demanded that any future problem be brought directly to me, stating that gossip was unproductive in solving matters and unfair until all facts were confirmed. Glaring at them, I offered the chance for comments. As there were none, I closed the meeting. When leaving, they all rather sheepishly shook my hand, and left immediately for home without the usual after meeting chat.

As the last car disappeared, my legs turned to jelly and I collapsed into a chair. Walking home down the bush track that night I felt a glow, knowing I had learnt a valuable lesson concerning teacher/parent and teacher/community relationships.

One morning my car broke down. Luckily, I managed to arrange for the postmistress to stop the bus and let the children know I would be late.

Arriving at the school gate right on morning recess time, I was delighted to see the children filing in orderly manner out to recess, with Gr. 7 Roma's strident voice ringing in their ears.

"And don't run until you're right outside!"

As I entered the school she was already preparing for the next session.

"Jamie picked the lock like you do when you leave the school key at home, Sir. They had morning talk, and did their writing, spelling and arithmetic, and it's all corrected."

"Thank you, Miss Campbell. You are a marvel."

My compliment produced a pleased blush. As she turned to leave, I mimicked her strident voice, "And don't run until you're right outside."

She rewarded me with a self-conscious grin.

My time in that first rural school proved successful in several ways. Although obviously not all my doing, but maybe I did contribute to the result, most of the pupils became worthy and successful adults, and sixty years later, several remain valued friends of mine.

As well, I added much to my philosophy of teaching via my experiences, and also, of course, via some mistakes. Probably it could be said that my philosophy was now close to completed. Before beginning teaching, my theories were almost complete, but, as you learn every day, they had been slightly modified and polished.

Due to the experience with the inspector, one more was added. I became convinced that the needs of the children, as I saw them, must be my number one priority. Opinions and demands of people in authority, or of parents, would never make me deviate from this aim, if I felt their demands were contrary to these needs.

My theories now provided a solid basis for my teaching, but one niggle remained in my mind. I was not happy with my teaching of reading. The old story of the inspector asking the child to read aloud from the grade reader troubled me.

When asked by the inspector to read from the grade reader, the child answered, "I left my reader at home, sir, but if you tell me what page, I can read it anyway."

The availability of material for children was far from being satisfactory. The small set of bookshelves that held half a dozen scruffy books nowhere near filled the need. I remembered how I had thirsted for something new to read as a child myself. Then there was nothing at school other than the class reader and the monthly school paper, and very little had changed since. Like this school, we'd had a few books scrounged by teachers on a shelf at the back of the room, mostly uninspiring volumes. *Biggles* books from the almost as limited Sunday

School library, and the Champion comic, with its written stories rather than picture comics had helped for me a little, but I had still searched for more. I even read Dad's red-leather bound classics, *"Les Miserables"*, *"The Tale of Two Cities"*, *"Oliver Twist"*, etc., with their rice paper pages and their miniature print with no pictures.

At the age of eleven I was given *"Headhunters of the Coral Sea"* by Ion L. Idriess, the first book that I owned. It was a hard-covered large book – I treasured it and read it from cover to cover fourteen times. Twelve months later I was given *"The Great Trek"*, also by Ion L. Idriess, which I read eleven times.

It was thus with delight that a few years later I welcomed the introduction of new teaching techniques for reading and the graded reading schemes. You will read more of this later.

****

CHAPTER 5

A HEAD TEACHER TO GUIDE ME.

My next school was situated in a building that was of the new modern style, with flat roof, large windows and of concrete brick structure, a far cry from my little one-roomed weatherboard school set in the bush. It was a four-teacher school. The principal taught Grades 5&6, I taught Grades 3&4, an inexperienced young lady taught Gr. 2, and the head Teacher's daughter taught the Prep and Grade 1. The two extremities had separate classrooms, but Grade 2 and my grade shared a double room separated by a folding door, or perhaps I should say what should have been a folding door. The roof of this flash modern nine-year-old building, had already dropped so far that the doors would not move from their firmly folded extremities. Thus, the only barrier that separated the very noisy grade two from my sixty-four composite 3-4 children was a curtain, which only reached halfway to the ceiling. My children almost had to learn to lip-read

To my philosophy, I added the head teacher's decree on corporal punishment. On my first day, he made it very clear.

"Do you use the strap, Don?" he asked.

"I do, yes," I answered, "but only occasionally when absolutely justified – mainly for bullying."

"You have my permission to use the strap in this school," he began, "but never in anger. I insist that you count slowly to ten before using it."

I happily agreed.

One day he entered my room, followed by a new pupil, the most extraordinary child I had ever seen. He was a thirteen-year-old, huge, with an enormous mane of bright ginger thick hair. I deliberately refer to it as a mane as it covered his head and grew out of his neck right down beyond his collar. I immediately noticed that his pale-skinned, freckled fingers were well browned with nicotine stain.

"Billy is our new pupil, Mr Roberts," he said, pushing Billy forward. "His father is an itinerant worker. I cannot afford to have him in my room as too often I have to leave it to attend to office matters, and, to put it mildly, he can't be left unsupervised, so he is yours."

My mind flew into rapid mode. He was twice the size of any of my children and, as I correctly guessed, extraordinarily strong, thus possibly a danger to his classmates. It was on the tip of my tongue to argue the wisdom of this decision, but, taking one look at the lad, I changed my mind.

"I'll bet he has faced the situation of not being wanted many times," I thought. Quickly I changed tack and put my arm around his shoulder.

"Hello, Billy," I said. "We will be delighted to have you in our grade."

After introducing him to the children I found him a seat near the front.

He beamed happily.

The children followed my lead and made him welcome. The head teacher approached me at recess and apologised for palming the lad off onto me.

"He has been here before, and is a very disruptive influence. You'll have to watch him very closely. I'll support you when I can," he warned.

As it turned out the lad proved to be happy and co-operative, although I had to watch him closely in the playground, as he didn't know his own strength and occasionally hurt another child unintentionally.

Billy stayed at our school for three months, which was a little stressful for me. As well as having to watch him so closely, he was way behind the class academically, so I had to accommodate that with a separate program of schoolwork and non-academic activities. With sixty-four other children in two grades, I had enough on my plate without having to cater for Billy.

While he was with us, the school dentist arrived. He travelled the state and checked all children's teeth once or twice during their primary years. When he entered my room to explain his program he caught sight of Billy.

"Oh no!" he wailed. "What have I done to deserve this?"

"You've met Billy before, have you?" I chuckled.

"Met him, yeah, head on." he sighed. "We had him at a school we visited last year. He succeeded in terrifying my nurse and totally wrecking my treatment van."

"If you checked him last year, perhaps you won't need to this year," I consoled.

"Despite our extended battle, I still didn't manage to get his mouth open, let alone inspect his teeth," he moaned.

The nurse duly came for Billy.

Not long after, a wild-eyed Billy careered back through the classroom door, raced to his seat, and sat, gripping that desk hard, defying anyone to try to take him back.

A rather dishevelled looking nurse, who arrived behind him, explained to me.

"We gave him enough sedative to subdue a bull elephant, and still he defeated us, and again wrecked the place. He has won." She added with conviction. "His teeth can remain unexamined!"

How glad I was that I was on friendly terms with Billy!

From my experience in this school I added one new theory to my teaching philosophy and modified two others.

Having sixty-four children in the room, sixty-five when Billy was with us, made it quite a task to learn and remember all their names. I noted the pleasure children displayed when I remembered their names and used them, and the disappointment if I could not. Obviously, it was important to them, so I decreed that in future I would learn the name of every child in my grade, no matter how many, by lunchtime on the first day I taught them. I would explain my aim to them, mention the difficulty of my task, and enlist their assistance, which they were always thrilled to give. During the first morning, I would read the names from the attendance register and each child would stand and say, "I am Jenny," or whatever the name was. I would repeat the name and we would have a short chat, with me using that name during every sentence. On the second time around, each child would stand in order and give me a hint, the first letter and some other clue, if I needed it. After that round I would ask each to stand and I would guess the name. Thumbs up told me I was correct and thumbs down meant I had to try again. They loved the routine and it proved successful in every way.

In larger schools, I learnt almost every name in the school, although it took longer to achieve. It helped greatly in building rapport, which led to general respect and co-operation.

To the theory on corporal punishment, I added that it should never be delivered in anger. A slow count to ten was a successful way of guaranteeing this.

My experience with Billy caused me to add another clause to my theory that every child should feel useful and successful in at least one activity. A child must also feel welcome, even wanted.

Having to contend with the deafening noise from the other side of the curtain, I also became convinced that a modulated working noise was okay in a classroom, but an over-noisy room was totally counter-productive. I knew for certain that a quiet teacher voice was the best way of achieving this.

****

Chapter 6

A ONE-TEACHER SCHOOL AGAIN.

My next school was another small one-teacher school, which was blissfully devoid of major problems.

Parent/teacher relationship and co-operation was an area of which I had already learned much. A friendly parent quietly confided to me that the over-enthusiastic school committee secretary, an overweight farmer parent, loved his role, but was inclined to want to make all policy decisions for the school.

Faced with this situation, I carefully explained to him that I was trained to run a school and could and would do it successfully. I would welcome his input, but decisions on all matters pertaining to teaching were for me to make. Slightly confronted at first, he came around to it eventually, and we developed an excellent working arrangement.

On the first day, I received convincing confirmation for my belief that a teacher should be his natural self, and should be happy to laugh heartily in front of the children if a situation tickled him, especially if the joke were on him. When a Gr. 4 girl arrived home after the first day of school that first year I was there, her mother asked her what she thought of the new teacher.

Enthusiastically she replied, "He's terrific. He laughs."

Less than a month after my arrival the combined small schools' swimming carnival was held. Recruiting two mothers I transported the children to the nearest swimming pool eleven miles away and tested their abilities at swimming. I managed to place every child into an event, except nine-year-old Rory. The carnival had an excellent scoring system. The winner scored four points for his or her school. The second placegetter scored three points, third scored two points and every child who completed the race scored a point. This generated great enthusiasm amongst the children, and every child who scored a point received generous applause plus back slapping from peers.

Rory could hardly swim a stroke, in fact he struggled to stay afloat, let alone progress. There was no way he could dive in the deep end and safely negotiate the thirty-metre distance to the finish line, so I was forced to leave him off the list.

He gazed aghast when the list was posted on the notice board and he could not find his name.

"Mr Roberts!" he cried out in mortification, "you forgot me!"

"I left you out Rory, because the swim is too long for you, and you are not permitted to let your feet touch the bottom. I'll teach you to swim during the year and you can swim next year." I hoped the promise would comfort him.

"But sir," he persisted, "I gotta swim. You get a point for your school."

What could I say? I hesitated, but I was forced to add his name by the other children unanimously and insistently pleading,

"Let him swim, Sir!"

There would be no risk as I was the appointed lifesaver for the day and would watch him closely.

Came the great day. The children had to sit within their school's designated roped off area, and only leave it to go to the start of their race. As I was busy with life-saving duties a mother supervised my children. Excitement ran high. We managed a few placegetters and they had all finished, triumphantly scoring their point.

Then came Rory's race. He stood there on the blocks, tiny, shivering and obviously petrified. I felt for him and gave him a few words of comfort. Bang went the starter's gun, and in dived the line of swimmers, that is, all the competitors except Rory. Had he frozen with fear at the last moment? No, he was just working out how to enter the water – he couldn't dive. Finally working it out, he sat on the edge and slid in. His opponents all powered down the pool to yells of support from their peers. By the time they had all reached the finish line and climbed out, Ronny had splashed his way about five metres, and was slowing down even further. I called encouragement to him and reminded him to yell or raise one arm if he needed me. Unexpectedly, I was drowned out by a noise. My children had suddenly broken ranks and had run to the pool's edge. Sitting on the edge of the pool, they kicked the water vigorously, chanting "Ror-ry! Ror-ry!" at the top of their lungs. I did nothing to stop them. There are times for rules to be forgotten.

To my delight, within moments, every child from every other school also broke ranks, and joined my children around the edge of the pool, kicking water and joining in the chant. No teacher attempted to stop it. Parents and teachers were even moved to join the chant.

Rory struggled on, most certainly buoyed by this extraordinary support. Inch by tortuous inch he progressed. I thought he would never reach the finish line, but he had different ideas. Eventually he touched the finish and I lifted him out of the water, and held him high to tumultuous cheers.

"I scored the Point, Sir!"

"I got our point, Mr Roberts," he gasped.

"You sure did Rory and we're really proud of you."

He sighed, contented.

What did I learn from this? Firstly, I learned to have faith in children, and, of course never, ever underestimate them. Perhaps also, I learned that for extraordinary circumstances, you should occasionally allow rules to be bent a little. Given the incentive and encouragement, children can achieve far beyond their normal limits, and the power of peer groups is almost unlimited.

A new prep child arrived in a car with his mother at the start of the second year. He refused to leave the car when his mother opened the door. From a distance, I noticed her predicament. He kicked and hit her, all the time screaming abuse. This was far more than nervousness – he was getting away with being a brat. The mother was about to give in and take him home, when I arrived on the scene. Grabbing him by the arm I lifted him out.

"Go home now, Bev," I instructed the mother, adding, "and don't worry about him. He will be fine when you have gone."

He was, after I suggested he join the other children in their games. On the next morning, the performance began as on the day before, but immediately ceased as the boy noticed me heading towards him. After a few more similar arrivals he opened the car door himself and jumped out. Happily waving to his relieved mum, he raced in through the gate to join the other children.

Crisis over.

Doing the almost impossible is not necessarily confined to children. It concerned me that the school building was surrounded by a small patch of asphalt, another patch of bare clay and a large paddock of long dry grass, hardly a welcoming aspect for children, and a haven for snakes. It was necessary for me to keep a snake charmer (a length of twisted number eight wire), hanging by the door, and to use it to keep the children safe. What a difference an attractive well-kept garden and a young farmers experimental crop would make. With a plan in mind, I approached the school committee with what I felt was an attractive proposal.

"I would dearly love to plant a garden around the school for both aesthetic and educational purposes, and form a young farmers' club," I spruiked during a committee meeting. "If we sank a bore, all that would become possible. Old Joe DeVaus is a water diviner of renown as you all know, and he assures me he would find good water."

They smiled benevolently at my naivety.

The chairman acted as their spokesperson. "We applaud the idea and your plans, but sinking a bore is a very expensive operation. A small school and sparsely populated district like ours could never find the money to fund it."

They did have a point, as the local hall had hosted no more than a small weekly euchre group for twenty years. In more remote places, the local hall became the community hub, hosting dances, meetings and other activities. This community was too close to the facilities and activities of a large town, and the local hall was almost unused.

However, I persevered, and explained the details of my plan. They eventually agreed to carry out the project if I could raise the money.

I played football for a team fifteen miles away. By recruiting my team members and the football club's supporters, I managed to form a band and gain the services of some talented entertainers. My children made beautiful posters advertising our dance, and I arranged for them to display their posters prominently in the large town eleven miles away.

When the great night came, I could hardly believe my eyes. Cars streamed through the gate in an almost unbroken line, until the hall was so packed the people overflowed, many chatting outside. It was a raging success with many queries as to when the next one would take place. We conducted it monthly, and very soon the bore project was fully funded and went ahead as planned. The one flaw was we had no electricity, but it was promised at the beginning of the following year, so, instead of installing a windmill, the committee decided to wait the six months and install the more reliable electric pump. Unfortunately, I gained promotion and left just before it was installed. More unfortunate still, the teacher who followed me was not inspired to carry out the projects I had planned, so the only benefit was water laid on to his residence, which was next door to the school.

This project made it clear to me that a teacher can be far more than the person who stands out in front of a classroom of children.

I have talked previously of the shortcomings of some district inspectors, so it is satisfying to record a compliment. Towards the end of the first term, the inspector arrived for his inspection. At the conclusion, he said in a confidential manner, "Don, I have many teachers of one-teacher schools in my inspectorate. Most of them are young, immature and inexperienced, so I like to give them guidance. They need someone to advise them, help solve their problems and bolster their confidence. The task is too big for just me, so could you fulfil that role for the schools in your vicinity. At twenty-three years of age, I was not sure I had the qualification for the task, but accepted. The role developed into friend, teaching advisor, and in some cases psychologist and personal relationship advisor.

It seemed that experienced teachers needed to be an example and a guide to other teachers.

****

Chapter 7

CITY BOUND

To gain promotion to a country school with a residence can take a very long time, so I borrowed money, bought a house in Melbourne and took my first promotion.

I had to drive across several suburbs to my school, but it was workable. The school was situated in a housing commission flats district, with all the associated problems of such an area. Although I personally experienced no disciplinary problems at the school, the children, who gathered in large numbers in a confined area after school, quite unsupervised until hotel closing at 6.00pm, ran riot, causing much strife. Their actions ranged from an organised boy/girl sexual relations group, which had a deserted hut as its centre of operation, to activities like burning two buses, during the three years I taught there. A well organised after-school program was badly needed to cater for this situation, but people to run it were not available. I wished I could take it on, but living some distance away in a house on a virtual paddock that desperately needed fences, carport and patio built and landscaping done, I was rather hamstrung. Add to that, having a wife, a young child and another on the way. Despite this heavy program, I did coach the girls' softball team one night a week and once a month I organised the older children to perform activities to benefit the school. One task they enjoyed was creating a garden and tending it. Also, as the school-ground was bereft of trees we worked out where they would best serve both beautification and shade, and planted them. Obviously, this was but a drop in an ocean to what they needed, but it was something.

While at the school, I was recruited to be one of a small group of teachers to experiment with the impending new approach to maths, which was based around the use of Cuisenaire Rods, and aimed at developing understanding of the number system and mathematical processes.

All my life I had been capable at maths, as I was blessed with a good memory, but one thing had always bothered me a bit. I accepted, but never understood why, if you multiplied by a whole number it made more, and if you divided by a whole number it produced less, but if you did the same with a fraction the results were the opposite. One day I was teaching a child division using the rods, when suddenly I called out, "Eureka, I've got it!" Suddenly I understood it all clearly, thus became a strong advocate for the use of concrete materials for teaching maths, and gave the changes the thumbs up. It was adapted for use in all Victorian schools the following year, but before long the more sophisticated multi-attribute blocks replaced the Cuisenaire Rods.

This involvement led to me to becoming enthusiastic about new and advanced methods of teaching, with dramatic changes to the teaching of reading following close on the heels of the maths.

It was a period of great changes in teaching, all of which had merit, but unfortunately were often introduced with insufficient training for teachers, resulting in faults in the system developing, and some teachers refusing to make any change. Human nature resists change, which can only be satisfactorily brought about in education circles if teachers clearly understand the necessity for it, and are confident in their knowledge of the change and where it is heading. I followed the introduction of this new maths with interest and noted one weakness in particular. Most teachers adopted the understanding approach quite well, but many now ignored the need for their children to also know number facts and tables. I made a feature of this neglected section, but, remembering how I found it fun competing with my brother as kids while we dried the dishes, I taught the number facts and tables, not with the boring old repetition method, although we did a little of that, but mainly through games and competitions. The children loved them, and not only did they learn the material, but proudly became fast at it.

Having had serious concerns about my teaching of reading, I welcomed with relish the new sentence method, which involved learning by reading whole sentences, which were of interest to the children, rather than by the phonic and word recognition method. As anything that caught their attention occurred in the classroom, we would compose a sentence about it and either I, or often one of the children, would write that sentence on one of the strips of white cardboard I had ready waiting. This would be displayed with the many others around the classroom, and often read, with little competitions based on recognising individual words within those sentences. This activity greatly improved their vocabulary recognition and did so surprisingly quickly. As with the new maths, though, one thing troubled me. What were we teaching to help their word attack when they came across a new word?

Teachers seemed to be completely ignoring this need and teaching phonics became a lost art. I spent considerable time teaching phonics alongside the sentence method. The results proved this double approach to work very well.

****

CHAPTER 8

NORTH TO THE WARMTH

After three years in Melbourne we had to move north, as our children suffered from bronchial asthma. Most of these new approaches, I developed further during my four years at this school.

Arriving at the school a few days early to do some early preparation before school began, I was struck by the beauty of the place. Two giant jacaranda trees stood between the school with its garden, and a small vineyard within the school- ground. If the school was as good as its surroundings it would be a great place at which to work. At lunch-time I slipped over to the corner store nearby for a bite of lunch. Before the door closed behind me a voice behind the counter display said,

"I don't believe it."

To our mutual amazement, the body that emerged from where it had been hidden, proved to be that of my old football coach of the team which I had recruited to raise money for the bore at my last one-teacher school.

"I hope you still play football," he continued.

"No, too old like you," I responded.

"Well, never mind. We can still use you. I am a committee man, selector, and specialist coach of the backline. You can fill all three roles too, except we will have you coach the on-ballers. You will have a valuable input."

I mention that, to point out that, as well as teaching children, a teacher must also be active in the local community.

An interesting situation arose early after school began. The headmaster called a staff meeting. He had been a sergeant major in the army, a fact that became very clear by the way in which he ran his school. Every day of the year, despite the extremely hot summer, he wore a suit, collar and tie, and marched briskly around the school in highly polished leather-soled shoes. Both children and teachers could fortunately hear his approach from some distance away. The teachers found something to do that clearly demonstrated their diligence, and the children sat noticeably straighter and suddenly became model hard working pupils at the distinctive sound of his approach.

At this afore-mentioned meeting, he informed the teachers that he made all the decisions affecting the school, and these decisions would be obeyed promptly and to the letter. His methods, he informed us, were proven over many years, and he ran the tightest and best school around. Discipline in his school was unquestioned and punishments severe. Teachers would teach English by the time-honoured method of formal grammar, analysis, and parsing, and maths would be taught by rote learning of tables number facts and the processes. Furthermore, he would personally test throughout the school every two months, correct it all, and expected results to satisfy him and indicate that his instructions had been followed to the letter.

"My personal specialty is poetry, which I, myself, will teach in every room from grades 3-6, demanding high standards of elocution throughout," was his final decree.

I could not believe the demands I was hearing, nor the meek acceptance of them by all the staff. The teachers were rather stunned and speechless, but accepting, as the head teacher fully expected. He was outraged when I calmly reacted quite differently.

"Your methods were current in the days of Adam, and much progress has been made since. I know one room that will not be teaching anything like your way. It would be setting my teaching back at least thirty years."

His reactions indicated that he had never before, in his entire life, been defied. Just for a moment or two he was lost for words. Then he exploded.

"Are you suggesting that the methods I have proven over many years don't work?"

"I'm sure they achieve your aims, which would appear to be to pound facts into children's heads. My aims are to educate them, to teach them how to learn, to love learning, and thus want to continue doing so. I want to ensure they thoroughly understand what they are learning. My aim also includes the development of their personalities and characters, and to give them initiative and self-confidence, so they can become independent learners. Would your methods achieve my aims?"

"Your class will be tested the same as the rest of the school, and they will be expected to pass grammar consisting of analysis and parsing. If they gain poor results you may well have to face irate parents."

"I would be very happy to do so," I assured him.

"We will discuss this further tomorrow after school in my office. See that you are there."

That discussion did take place, but 'argument' might be a more accurate word than discussion. Neither of us gave away any ground. From that day on he called me "The Rebel", and grudgingly let me have my own way.

It seemed that he found me a challenge, as almost every day he would initiate a discussion with me, usually beginning with,

"You would have to admit, Don ---." Following this would be something like, "that my poetry lessons produce excellent class recitation."

"I certainly do," I answered that particular claim, "but they also make children hate poetry."

"How do you justify that statement, when they recite it so beautifully?" he would ask.

"Because you murder the beauty of poetry. You recite a poem selected by you, one which you think would be suitable for expressive recitation. Whether the children might like it does not seem to be a consideration. Then taking it phrase by phrase, you force the children to repeat it over and over until they use your exact notation. You do nothing to help them enjoy it. In fact, when you leave the room, I take another poetry lesson to give poetry a chance."

"And what do you do differently?" he demanded to know.

"For a start, I read them a poem that I feel children of their age might enjoy, and ask them if they liked it or did not like it. We discuss why, and what they did or did not like. If it suggests some activity we can follow up like acting it, or illustrating it, we do that. If they really like it, we will enter it into their anthologies, and because they want to do it they take great care to do it well. Their real favourites we learn, but a verse at a time, not by meaningless short phrases."

"I don't imagine you manage to elicit the perfect elocution that I achieve," he boasted.

"Probably not, but nor do I have a classroom of totally bored pupils who hate poetry. I achieve my aims and you achieve yours. We are just on different planets."

Another day he would attack me on English expression.

"It is vital that they learn parts of speech, phrases, clauses, adjectives, adverbs etcetera, so they can write well, and for learning other languages in the future, that educating for the future, to which you often refer. You must agree to that, and parsing and analysis my way, teaches it to them."

"I also believe in them knowing their grammar," I said, much to his surprise. "But instead of tearing someone else's writing apart to learn it, I teach them to learn by using it to build interesting sentences themselves. We start with just a subject and verb, add an object, then make it say exactly what we mean by adding adjectives, adverbs, phrases and clauses. They first see the need, which is because they realise that I won't know exactly what they mean unless they add clarification, and they actually enjoy doing it to make things clear to me. How often have you heard some child say, 'Oh goodie! We are going to do analysis'?"

Our school was known as a hot-box school. The temperatures in summer hovered around the 100degrees F and often rose considerably higher. As there was no cooling system in these schools we were obliged to teach outside under a tree when the weather rose to 105F., and send the children home when it reached 108F. Despite the climate, all teachers and bankers in the district still wore long trousers and collar and tie all year round. Finding this ridiculous, I began wearing shorts, open neck shirts and long socks, very sensible and neat apparel. As expected, reaction proved dramatic.

"What teaching assessment are you on, Don?" asked my head teacher. In those days each teacher received an annual visit by the district inspector, who awarded an assessment from unsatisfactory, through good, very good, to outstanding.

Warily I answered, "Why do you ask?"

"It's important," he insisted.

"All right – it's the top one," I informed him.

"Outstanding is of great benefit to a teacher's future," he continued. "You do realise that if the inspector sees you dressed like that, he will downgrade you."

"If he does, then it's not worth the paper it's written on," I retorted.

Although I continued wearing that apparel until the weather cooled, I survived the heat of every variety, and the inspector did not downgrade my assessment.

The following year most men teachers and nearly all the bankers in the district wore shorts, open neck shirts and long white socks.

I noticed the boss calling into my classroom quite often to see how I was teaching various subjects, but not once during that year did he concede that my teaching might be as effective as his, nor even that it might have some value for the children.

The end of the year arrived, and he allotted classes for the following year. In typical fashion, he regarded this as his role alone. One new teacher was arriving, a twenty-year-old man.

When I read the new class lists, I stormed down to his office. He had allotted fifty-nine grade 5 children to me and given nineteen grade 4 & 5 children to the new man.

"If you wish to punish me for not toeing your line, you don't have to insult the new bloke and disadvantage so many children to do it," I began, quite ready to fight his unfair attack.

"I am the Head Teacher of this school," he stated firmly, "and feel no compulsion to explain my decisions to you, Don, but in this case, I will. Firstly, I have no information on the teaching ability of the new chap. Secondly, as it happens, I feel that as many children as possible should benefit from having you teach them for a year."

This time I was quite lost for words. Not once in twelve months had he given any credence to my methods, and here he comes out with an incredible statement like that.

How do you fathom such a man? He left the school a year later, still not having offered me one more word of commendation or agreement.

Every child is important and any special needs deserve a teacher's attention.

Ron in Grade 4 was brilliant academically. One day he raised his hand tentatively and nervously said,

"I'm afraid you are wrong, sir."

Wrong to Ron was a devastating experience. He made only one mistake in maths for the year and sat, fretting about having done so for a full half an hour. I wanted to show him that a mistake is not the end of the world, so I replied quite cheerfully.

"If I am it would not be the first time, Ron. Everyone makes mistakes, and sometimes that is a good thing as you can learn from a mistake. Would you explain where I was wrong to the class and to me, please?"

"Well, Sir." Here he repeated my earlier comment. "In the library, there is a set of knowledge books. In volume 5 on page159 it says you are wrong."

I was fairly sure I knew that set of books to which he was referring. Its pages had two columns, so I rather facetiously asked, "Which column, Ron?"

"The second column, sir," he answered taking me seriously.

So that he could feel important I asked him to borrow the book and read the article to us.

Of course, he was correct in every detail. In answer to my curiosity he admitted that he had read it during library period three weeks earlier.

I said he was a genius. Obviously, I could do little to assist his brain, but perhaps I could help him in other areas. Socially he was a bespectacled loner, and was hopeless at sport, in which he showed total disinterest. In these two areas, perhaps I could help.

After considering the situation, I said to him one day, "Do you know, Ron, that it is a proven fact that exercise and sport assist students in their studying of academic subjects?"

I intended leaving that thought with him, but he immediately came back to me with,

"Did it actually help you, Sir?"

"It certainly did, Ron. After two or three hours of study at night, my mind would become tired and my study ineffective. By speed skipping for twenty minutes, my mind would freshen and I could study well for another three hours."

"Interesting," mused Ron.

"Also interesting is that playing sport on Saturday made me feel refreshed and more like attacking my studies the following week," I added.

The next day, to my delight, I saw Ron playing kick to kick football with other children for the first time. Unfortunately, he was quite hopeless, sometimes even missing the ball. Obviously, my project was unfinished. After school, when the other children had gone home, I helped him. So dedicated was he that he improved rapidly, eventually playing in the first ruck for the district seconds team during his teens. Later, he even returned on weekends from university to play his football.

Wendy was not in my grade, but she was the sort of child you noticed. Although only in Grade 5, she was easily the tallest child, boy or girl, in the school. Her height had begun to embarrass her, and she had started to slouch. A tall girl or lady can be very attractive, but only if she carries her body straight. Bad posture not only looks dreadful, but is detrimental to health. I became concerned for her and looked for a chance to help her. After some fruitless thought, the solution suddenly occurred to me. She was a capable swimmer and diver, particularly the latter. One of our teachers was a tall, ex-district swimming champion, who had excellent posture.

"What do you think of Miss Dawe?" I asked Wendy one day.

"Oh, she's terrific!" she answered with enthusiasm.

Terrific was the in word at the time, so this was indeed high praise.

Casually I mentioned, "She tells me that her height and the fact that she carries herself so straight and tall, give her an advantage in swimming and diving."

She hadn't actually told me that, but a small white lie can be justified if it can help.

Imagine my pleasure when I noticed Wendy standing tall and proud at assembly the following day. While the iron was still hot I pressed my advantage.

"I will be coaching swimming at the pool tomorrow after school, Wendy. If your mother gives her permission I may be able to help you with your diving."

She was there waiting with a note of permission from her mother.

The story has a happy ending. She won the inter-school diving both that year and the following year. I have been told that she also grew to be an impressive looking six feet plus lady, who received many an admiring glance due to her height and erect posture.

When the head teacher moved after two years, Santa Claus replaced him. He had a large mop of snow white hair, a rosy red face, and a most gentle nature.

"I know nothing about being a head teacher, having been a classroom teacher all my working life" he freely admitted. "The only reason I applied for the position for my last two years of teaching was to increase my superannuation cheque on retirement. You people run the school and I will create a beautiful school garden."

That is exactly what happened. Although perhaps not the ideal situation, both teachers and children happily enjoyed an effective education.

The afore-mentioned twenty-year old teacher, could find no other place to board in the town, so we took him in, and a fourteen-year old lad from Murrayville, Elaine's home town had been boarding with us for two years, while doing his secondary education.

One day Elaine said rather crossly, "Rodney spends more time with our kids than you do."

That made me stop and think. After some reflection, I had to admit that she was quite right. I had let myself become Mr School, running everything at our own school and organizing all inter-school sports. Added to that I had also become Mr Community. A member of the Apex young men's service club, I was director of the overseas relations portfolio, and I regularly attended dinner meetings and working bees. One night a week, I ran a boys' club at the church and taught Sunday School on Sundays. As I had a great love for the game, I continued as a specialist coach, selector, and committee man of the football club, and had even made a comeback to playing. Of an evening, I played men's basketball in the winter months and bowls in the summer, and was an enthusiastic cricketer during the summer months. I'm exhausted just writing it all down. Although I was a good dad when time allowed, I obviously could not fill the role often enough.

It was not easy to just drop these activities, many being worthy. The best solution that occurred to me was to move, and what better than a move overseas. Perhaps there my time would not be in such demand.

Arriving home from school one day, I dropped my books onto the table and announced.

"I'm applying for an overseas position. Anyone coming?"

This may sound like a domineering male, but it was not at all. I knew well what the response would be.

"With bells on!" responded Elaine. "What took you so long?"

We applied for two islands and Butterworth Air Base in Malaysia, hoping for one of the islands, which was advertising for both a male and a female teacher.

Though each vacancy on this island had at least four hundred applications, we were lucky enough to both be appointed to a position – perhaps a husband/wife team suit them.

****

CHAPTER 9

ON A PACIFIC ISLAND - HOW DIFFERENT!

With much excitement, we prepared to leave. White shorts, open neck shirt and long white socks formed the school wear for men teachers. These were not available as it was in May, but this was the only real hitch.

One amazing thing happened two weeks before we were to sail. The ex-head-teacher, with whom I had constantly crossed swords, contacted me from Melbourne. Apparently, the education department had built a new 'you-beaut' school as a showpiece. He was one of a group of senior principals who had been asked to see that it was fitted with the best of furniture, equipment and every possible teaching requirement. They had also been asked to select a suitable principal and senior staff. Apparently, he had recommended that I be appointed the principal and had persuaded the others to agree. He pointed out that it would be a remarkable promotion from second-class assistant to first-class principal, jumping about fifteen years. He even gilded the deal by offering Elaine the position of librarian of the superbly equipped library, not really a concession on his part, as she ran an outstanding library that always became the hub of the school.

It was certainly tempting, and at any other time I wouldn't have hesitated to accept, but our hearts were all set on life on an island by this time, so I knocked it back. One sometimes wonders what life would have thrown up had we departed the revolving door of opportunity elsewhere, but I never regretted my decision.

The island administration packed our furniture and belongings, most of which was placed in storage, as our house there would be fully furnished.

On board one of the island's fleet of three ships, we met fellow passengers who worked for The British Phosphate Commission, and for the Island Administration, plus one native. The latter happened to not only be a teacher, but taught in the department of the school that would be under my supervision. Naturally I pumped him for information about the school and the children, but he was extremely shy and reluctant to communicate. All I could glean was that both teachers and children were eagerly, but apprehensively awaiting my arrival.

The first book I had ever owned as a child was Head Hunters of the Coral Sea, by Ion L. Iddriess. Ever since reading it, I had dreamed of the romance of peaceful lagoons protected by coral reefs. As we approached the island I received a shock. Where were the lagoons and the coral reef? It seemed there were none. There was a coral reef, but it adjoined the narrow strip of stony sand and projected fifty metres out to sea before dropping sixty fathoms sharply to the sea floor.

With no pier or even a jetty in sight I asked another passenger how we landed.

"You climb down a fragile metal stairway, which the sailors will attach to the side of the ship, and step onto a barge. That is unless the captain decides it is too rough, in which case we are lowered into the barge in a net by a deck crane."

I looked down at the eight to ten feet waves on which the three small barges that had already arrived were pitching crazily, and was sure they warranted the crane. Wrong – the sailors were already preparing the stairway. Somehow, we safely negotiated this hazardous exercise, and crept into the calm water of the concrete-walled boat harbour. Gratefully finding our feet on land at last, we were met by our school principal in his air-conditioned Mercedes, bought duty-free on the island. On the way to our house we passed our schools, mine a rambling one-storey structure and Elaine's school, which housed just grade two children, a smaller two-storey building which looked a little cooler.

Arriving early Saturday morning we soon settled in. As I had heard that the Education football team were playing Australian Rules football against the Police team, and teachers from my school would be playing, I went to watch the last half. All I really learned was that, although they were the more skilful, they either lacked stamina or determination, as they lost after leading well, even into the last quarter.

An episode that I felt at the time would have little bearing on my teaching probably needs to be recorded here. Those readers who have read my sport book, 'Weekend Warriors – The Games We Played', will know of it.

The teachers, some of whom played for the Education football team, pleaded with me to play for them. I first decided to have some fun with them to soften the blow of what I was determined to say in response to their plea. "The police team ran all over you in the last corner despite you being obviously the more capable team. Why would I want to play with a team that lacks stamina, or determination or both?"

"It was neither stamina nor determination," they stated. Then to my amazement one of them added, "We let them win. You don't beat the police team or you will be booked for something the next week."

I stored that valuable piece of information in the back of my brain.

Having retired for the second time the previous year, I had little desire to make yet another comeback at all, let alone in a tropical climate on a coral chip surface. Not wanting to offend them so early in my time with them, I finally agreed to their second choice, that of being an umpire. This decision I would regret.

The next Saturday, after only one week on the island, a local team was playing a team of Gilbert and Ellis Islanders, who were on the island on a five-year working contract. Knowing well the problems that could arise, the other umpires on the umpiring board appointed me to umpire the match. I knew very little about the nature of the indigenous players, and nothing about what to expect from the others. Only later did I discover that there was considerable racial tension between the two teams.

I arrived very early for the game, but not as early as the players or the crowd, who impatiently awaited me, with the two teams lined up facing each other. In years gone by in Australia, when boots had nailed leather stops, they lined up like this for the umpire to rub soles to check for dangerous protruding nails. Moulded plastic stops had long since put a stop to this process. Not so here. The ritual was still quite definitely expected. Only six players out of the forty, even wore boots. Most were barefooted, a few wore thongs, and one wore socks and thongs. Try running in those, let alone kicking. He could.

To appease their obvious and eager expectation, I rubbed the soles of those first in line, who were the players wearing boots. Then I walked along behind the others, saying to each player as I passed.

"You're Okay."

This would not suffice at all. I was summarily called back, and dutifully rubbed all the dirty hard-skinned bare feet.

As I was the only official umpire, I recruited goal and boundary umpires from the milling crowd, guessing quite correctly, that I would have to watch closely for biased decisions.

Within seconds of the first centre bounce, the ball went out of bounds, so I called for the boundary umpire to throw it in. Checking carefully where his ruckman was, he deliberately threw the ball directly to his man's advantage. With no chance to reach the ball, the other ruckman chose to hit his opponent's head instead. Rising from the ground the ruckman who had been punched had murder in his eyes, whereas the offender was happy.

I made a quick decision. I had to calm the victim, not the offender. He was a giant of a man and I was 5 ft 7 ins tall and 9 stone 2 lbs wringing wet.

As he was rising, I wrapped my arms around his from the front, and spoke soothingly. Totally ignoring me, his attention entirely on his intended victim, he reached a vertical position with me dangling in front like a koala cub on the wrong side of its mother.

The next thing I knew, I was lying on the ground, looking up at the bearded brown face of a spectator, who had apparently hit me from behind as I was dangling. Shaking my head to gather my wits, I heard his angry accusation as he pointed at the opposing offending ruckman.

"Him, not him!"

He either didn't understand, or else vigorously disagreed with my reasoning.

Gazing briefly around, I found myself in the centre of a situation that threatened to get dangerously out of hand. All thirty-six players and five hundred plus spectators were all milling angrily around. No help was likely – it was up to me. Acting on instinct I searched for the football and my whistle, both of which were luckily close by. Tucking the former under my arm, I blew a mighty blast on the latter. To my great relief, the whole crowd momentarily paused. Taking advantage of the moment of silence, I yelled authoritatively, at the top of my voice.

"There will be no game of football!"

Having no experience of them I was gambling. I fervently hoped they would love a game of football more than a fight, or a feed of expatriate umpire.

Stunned faces stared unbelievingly at me.

I continued as sternly as I could.

"I will count to ten. If every spectator is outside the fence and every player in his right position by ten, we will play. If they are not, I take the football home and there will be no game."

Would it work, or would they tear me limb from limb?

In my loudest voice, which luckily was very loud, I began the count.

"One! Two! Three!" I ground out.

Not a single movement. It looked like goodbye cruel world. I wanted my mummy.

"Four!" I shouted.

Suddenly, one player turned and ran for his position. This triggered a stampede. Before I reached ten, all six hundred or so were where they were instructed to be, eagerly awaiting the restart of play.

During the next two hours, I nipped several more incidents in the bud, but, with bad cramp in both legs towards the end, I managed to keep the peace until the game was completed.

Why have I related this story?

It was not until well after the incident that I realised its importance, that it was another revolving door situation, which would have significant influence on my life, particularly for the next two years.

Football was about the most important activity in the lives of the islanders. Within a few hours, every indigenous person, man, woman and child, would have heard the story of the new teacher/umpire who tamed the angry mob and made them obey. What's more the story would probably have improved with every telling.

If he had done this, who were they, as individuals, to question his authority. I commanded respect from that time forward. If, however, I had departed the revolving door at a point of defeat or retreat, life in general, and particularly my teaching experience, might have been very different, perhaps even very difficult.

I was to teach a Grade 4 of twenty local native children and four expatriate children. As I had always related easily with a new grade, I looked forward to meeting them.

What a shock I had coming!

Their skin varied from very light brown to quite dark brown, and combined with jet-black hair and sparkling brown eyes, they looked a delight. However, the easy rapport I usually enjoyed with children was totally missing, so much so that they vehemently rejected all my friendly comments, scowling and unresponsive whenever I spoke to them, particularly if I spoke to a specific individual. The daughter of the teacher I had met on board ship, even pretended to spit on the floor when I spoke to her. I could hardly wait for morning recess so I could seek advice, particularly from the girl's father and other local teachers.

"The children seem aggro towards me," I said. "And your daughter almost spat on the floor when I made a friendly comment to her. Is there some secret to getting through to them?"

"The problem is that they are desperate for you to like them, but they are sure you won't. Until you can convince them that you do, you will get nowhere with them."

Though I thought I had been doing just that, I redoubled my efforts and laughed a lot, making sure I did not laugh at them.

One child shouted to me, "'Eey Robert! Look at Mary!" soon after recess.

"Mary hurt foot," she added, and everyone except Mary laughed. This seemed a strange reaction, but Mary's was even stranger."

"Have you hurt your foot, Mary?" I asked.

"No!" she answered furiously, then clarified further, "not hurt!"

I noted quite a deal of blood on the floor, so I asked her to show me her foot.

"No! Not hurt!" she snarled, pressing her foot hard onto the floor.

An elderly gentleman named David, was our liaison person. We had been told if any problem arose that we should contact him. I sent another child for David. When he arrived, it was obvious he had been told of the problem. He went straight to Mary. Ignoring her violent wriggling and shouted abuse directed at him, he lifted her unceremoniously, despite her wriggling, out of her desk. When her foot came into view, a large open cut was revealed on the underside.

"I'll deal with this, Don. Don't worry about her attitude. They hate to be singled out at any time, let alone if they are hurt, as all the other children will laugh at them."

How strange and how different from Australian children! I was learning that previous experience was of no value here. Teaching was a totally different game from what I had previously known – but I was learning fast.

When David returned, I broached him with another problem.

"I have two children here not listed to be in my grade, David. Could you check it out?"

"You probably have two missing also," he suggested.

"You're right," I admitted.

He asked me to point out the two boys and laughed when I did so.

"Quite often," he explained, "children decide to swap and live with another family for a while. They are never refused as everyone loves and spoils kids. Most families have about a dozen children, so another one here or there makes little difference. Those two have changed homes and have also changed their names to that of their new families. There's no problem."

By lunchtime, I had almost won them over, and was even rewarded with a shy smile or two.

During the lunch break I chatted with the other expatriate man teacher who taught grade 6.

"Many things you have to learn about them, Don, but two in particular. Firstly, they are extraordinarily shy and hate to be singled out, so you can't ask an individual child a question. They just won't answer if there is the slightest possibility that they might be wrong. The other children will all laugh at them if they make a mistake."

"I had just about worked that out," I told him and mentioned the incident with Mary."

"It would have been the same with any of them," he assured me. "I had one child who tried to hide the fact his leg was broken by dragging himself off to the nearest trees, despite the agony he must have been suffering. Always get David in such a circumstance.

The second thing you must know is that you cannot single out a child and force him to do something. He or she will never give in to your will. Kid to them and they will do anything for you, but don't butt your head against a brick wall by trying to force a child to obey. You will certainly lose every time."

Before lunch I had admired the girls' hair and the leis they wore on their heads. I did so, prompted by two things. The leis looked great, and if I took my eye off a girl for a moment, I might turn and hardly recognise her. In the blink of an eye they could completely change the appearance of their long, thick, black locks. Several of them wore head leis, some made of flowers, some of shells or coloured seeds.

When I returned from lunch, I found a dozen or more leis sitting neatly on my table. From this and other incidents, I learned to be careful about what I admired. Anything you said you liked became yours. They religiously followed the tradition of bubitze, which decreed that anything you liked had to become yours. An expatriate dentist owned a local mechanic's work vehicle, purely because he kindly admired it when he saw it. He had to agree to keep it in his garage every night, but persuaded the mechanic to collect it for work each day.

Much more I quickly learned. I enjoyed acting, which proved invaluable. Much could be explained to the children best by acting it. For example, during a silent reading session little Erica shouted, "'Eyy, Robert!" (I was always addressed that way if they wanted my attention) "What this 'terror'?" She was seeking the meaning of the word terror.

What better way to explain than to act it. I placed a child behind the door with instructions to jump out at me and say 'Boo!' when I entered the door. This caused me to jump back.

The performance brought much applause and shouts of "'Eyy! Terror!"

"No, that is not terror. That is fright," I explained.

"Aye! We know fright," came the response.

"That Terror, Robert?"

All the island native residents had a morbid fear of ghosts, so next I put a sheet over the hiding child.

"Ah, Ghost!" came the awed comments.

This time when the child jumped out saying 'Boo!" I shrieked and raced away, arms held high.

The applause was deafening and querying voices shouted, "That terror?"

"Aye," I responded. "That is terror."

They were satisfied and returned to their silent reading.

Another valuable aid was anything visual. When presented with something beyond their narrow island experience they refused to believe it unless they could see it in a picture or on a film. Fortunately, I had foreseen this possibility and come prepared with a wide range of large pictures. On one occasion, I was talking about farming, farming life, and how the phosphate their island exported was used. Comprehension of size was difficult for them, so when I claimed some Australian farms to be more than ten times the size of their whole island, I was greeted with an emphatic chorus.

"You lie, Robert!" they accused me.

Here a film eventually won their belief and sheer wonder. The highest land they had seen was their internal plateau, known as Topside, which rose about a hundred feet above sea level. Predictably, when I claimed that many mountains in the world were so high that their peaks rose way above the clouds, I was again greeted with the 'You lie, Robert!' response. Luckily, I had plenty of picture evidence.

All emotions were far more intense in these children than with Australian children. It was vital to take this into account when teaching them. In the early stages of my being with them, the children reacted differently from what I would have expected to various situations. Incidents that would make Australian children happy, island children would find hilarious. What might slightly annoy an Australian child, would make these children utterly furious.

Embarrassment would cause utter mortification. All these emotions were clearly on display. Interestingly, they could also change dramatically in a flash.

One day, just before morning recess, I did something that made the afore-mentioned, little Erica, extremely angry. She backed towards the door glaring viciously back at me and mouthing furious unmentionables under her breath. I felt it better to deal with it, than to let it stew all recess time, so I followed her, leaning forward and maintaining eye contact. Just before she reached the door I dropped her a big wink and grinned. Her transformation could not be understood unless experienced, but by this time I expected it. Her fury disappeared in a flash, immediately replaced by helpless laughter, pointing at me and saying "'Eyy, Robert!" which, expressed in that situation, was a sure sign of total approval. All disagreements were completely forgotten.

"EYY Robert! Tee Hee Hee."

One indigenous teacher, who was a Marshall Islander by birth, was the main singing teacher at the school. He taught singing with one hand holding a cornet to his mouth while in the other he grasped the strap, which was always at the ready. It was his responsibility to train a choir from the school to perform on stage for the island's independence celebrations. One day he approached me with a problem and a request.

"Don, I am striking problems with the choir practices. The kids keep disappearing out the door and running away. Could you spare the time to stand guard on the door?"

Of course, I did, and all went well until the Independence Ceremony. Unfortunately, I had to go back to Australia. My son, Doug, had suffered an infection in his ear. Due to the antibiotic not having been kept refrigerated properly, it had become ineffective and a hole had been left in his eardrum, requiring an operation. Apparently, the choir sang beautifully, but without my sheep-dogging influence, only one third of its members reached the stage. The rest escaped, scattering far and wide, at the last minute. However, that few apparently sang like little angels.

Part of my responsibility was to supervise the locally born teachers in Grades 3 and 4 during the first year. They had received only one year of training on the island, thus had some limitations. One of these teachers was outstanding – he had great rapport with his children and his teaching was sound. His only fault was that the day after their fortnightly payday, he never arrived at school due to having drunk his pay cheque. One problem I encountered was discipline, or rather lack of it.

Discipline in families was the total responsibility of grandfathers. Mothers and fathers just loved and enjoyed their children, taking no responsibility for discipline. Due to a dearth of grandfathers caused by so many men having been killed during Japanese occupation, when they had been shipped away to be work gangs on the island of Truk, discipline was almost non-existent in many homes. Because of this we faced two problems at the school. Firstly, the teachers sometimes did not bother to maintain discipline in the classroom. When they did, it was in the form of rather violent corporal punishment, which was more counter-productive, than effective.

Soon after my arrival, I glanced out of my door to see if all was well. It wasn't. Children in a Grade 4 were running riot, making a terrible din and jumping across desktops. Total bedlam reigned. Thinking that the teacher must have left the room for some reason, I raced to the room and took over. Finally regaining order, I turned, and, to my amazement, there at the table was the teacher. His chair tipped back and, his feet on the table, he was smoking and reading a comic book, while a child was scratching his shirtless back through the rails of the chair.

Once the children were settled and working on the maths as they should have been doing earlier, I took the teacher out of the room and explained how unprofessional and unproductive it was to let his class behave as they had been. I specifically mentioned that he should never smoke or read comics in the classroom. He politely accepted the criticism and agreed to change his ways and make sure the children were kept occupied.

At a similar time the next day, I checked him again. He had certainly changed his ways. With his shirt on he was standing in the doorway to his room holding his cigarette and comic carefully so they were just outside the doorway. Occasionally he would pause from his reading and smoking to glance back into the room. While checking on the slightly less bedlam than on the previous day, that reigned therein, he was careful to keep his cigarette and comic just outside. He wasn't really being contrary or rebellious, just following my instructions in a fashion that suited him.

The following year three new Australian men teachers were appointed. They were all outstanding teachers and strong personalities, so we four men each took charge of a grade level. Being the most experienced, I took over the Grade 6, which was a most important period in the education of the children, as, at the end of that year they sat for the scholarships to go to Australia for their secondary schooling. As well as teaching them, you had to prepare them for the possibility of going to Australia the following year.

From the start, I faced a problem that I had never before experienced. Singing was an important part of my teaching. I took it as a lesson, but often used it informally before, during, and after other subjects. These children refused point blank to sing for me. When I asked them why, they simply replied,

"We shy."

As far as they were concerned that was the end of the matter. It was far from the end for me. I knew they were very musical – all Pacific islanders of all ages were both musical, and had a wondrous body rhythm.

What a waste for them to not sing, particularly when I knew they loved to do so! Sitting outside during the night with everyone singing was a common occurrence in every village. A possible solution finally occurred to me – I devised a scheme. Unbeknown to them I set up a recording machine so I could start it from my table. I then placed my deliberately out of tune ukulele casually on the front desk of the girl who was the natural leader in the class, saying,

"I will be busy for a while. You may do what you like, as long as you stay in your seats and are not too noisy."

They were stunned, and at a loss for what to do. Something like this had never previously happened. For a while they sat in silence while I ignored them and pretended to be working at my desk. Before long I heard the quiet 'plunk, plunk, plunk, plunk' of the strings on my ukulele being checked. Then silence again to test the water. I completely ignored them and worked diligently. Soon I heard the strings being plucked again, nearer to being in tune, and finally, once more, this time in tune. Silence again and still I ignored them. By now they were starting to feel that I was not even with them.

After another short pause, Tina, the lass with the ukulele, started singing very quietly. She sang beautifully, but only for a brief period, then waited to see if I responded.

I didn't.

Now she began to feel confident and her voice grew stronger. When I still ignored it all, others began to drift in, singing the melody with her, with many adding harmony, everything from descants to base lines. I had heard this from adults on many occasions, as no doubt the children had too, but I had never heard it from children. Their talent had to be heard to be believed. They sang lilting island songs, both in their own language and English, including one of my favourites. A few lines of this song were :-

Silver waves are sighing
Softly on the shore,
While the stars are gleaming,
And we kissed once more.
Night fades, dawns another day,
Down by Illawari Bay.

Unfortunately, these words accurately typified their lifestyle. The climate caused night time to be far more pleasant than daylight hours, and whole villages often stayed up most of the night to enjoy it.

This we had to take into account in the school. The day's program would begin at 7.30 am, with a two-hour siesta lunch break at 12 noon. All basic subjects were taught during morning sessions, as several children just wanted to sleep during the heat of the afternoon. The afternoon session was mainly for art, music and physical activities.

After they had sung for some time, I raised my head.

"That was so beautiful to hear," I said, smiling.

A few grunts and mumbled responses came, but I took no notice of them.

"Would you like to hear yourselves?" I asked.

"We hear – when we sing," came from several throats.

"Listen," I suggested, and played the recording back to them. Looks of wonder and delight lit up their faces, accompanied by approving cries of "Aye! Aye! and even by clapping of hands.

I had won. They never refused to sing for me again, and we made magical music.

My Grade 6 was slightly noisier than I liked one day, so I spoke to the brightest girl in the class.

"Pattie," I said, "These children don't seem to understand what, 'keep quiet', means."

By now I had everyone's curious attention.

"How would I say it in your language? Perhaps they would understand that."

Normally they would not teach us their language, saying that, as only three thousand people in the world spoke it, it would be a waste of effort learning it. Anyway, they could all speak English for communication, so it was a waste of time. Another reason, I felt, was that they enjoyed being able to make comments in front of us without us understanding. Often, however, it was rather easy to guess by the tone of voice and facial expression. The word 'Suh!' undoubtedly meant the same as an English four-letter word beginning with the same letter.

This time, however, Pattie obliged.

"You would say, 'Bwicka yonen!'" she explained. With exaggerated expression in her voice, she added, "But that more like, 'Shut up you kids!' than 'Be quiet children.'"

"Aha! That's just what I want!" I thanked her.

Everyone laughed and got the message.

Having gained independence, the islanders started to make their own decisions, one of the first being the appointment of a new director of education. This type of decision had always been made for them in the past, and, because of this, they lacked the experience to make wise appointments. The man they appointed was an ex-airforce group-captain, whose experience was organising adult education. He was now responsible to head eleven kindergartens, a grade 2 school, a primary school and a junior high school. He lacked the knowledge, but would never admit it, and expected military type obedience to his commands from brilliant teachers in each field. The situation was primed for conflict.

Realising the unsuitability of the island's primary courses, which were copied word for word from the Victorian State's Course of Study, the dedicated primary staff had given up their first term holiday fortnight and totally re-written the courses to make them appropriate to the island situation. The new director arrived the following week. After being on the island only a few days, he called a meeting of the primary staff and aggressively made his demands. His opening statement was a bombshell.

"The primary courses are totally unsuitable for island children. You will begin re-writing them tomorrow and have them in my hands in one month's time."

The teachers to whom he made this statement were not only the best with whom I had ever taught, but were of a rather volatile temperament. I feared the consequences, so quickly took the initiative.

"Obviously, an educator of your standing would never make such a statement without having carefully studied the courses," I stated, a little tongue in cheek. "We need you to tell us in detail the areas where they are inadequate and what changes you would suggest we make."

"We don't have time for that in this meeting," he blustered.

"It is blatantly clear that you have not read them." I accused him. "I suggest you do so before you make any more uniformed and foolish comments." At emotional moments, I have been known at times, to lack tact.

Realising the hair on my neck was already standing on end, our head teacher interrupted to prevent outright war, in which all the other teachers were itching to join.

"Perhaps we should leave this matter until after the director and I have discussed it."

We never heard another word about it.

With impending independence, some of we expatriates started an Apex Young Men's Service Club, to give some of the younger islanders leadership experience, and develop a responsibility for the overall wellbeing of the community. They were most enthusiastic, but often did not turn up at the last minute, even if they had agreed to filling a role that night.

An interesting situation arose that indicated clearly that independence should not have been granted. One teacher, a very intelligent young man, often asked me questions about government and the future of the island. One day he approached me with an extraordinary question.

"Don," he said, "I have all this phosphate royalty money that I want to spend. Can you think what I could buy?"

Now, I knew that he and his young family slept outside their house, one of the houses the administration supplied free to every family. They could not sleep inside, as so much electronic equipment in the house left no room for sleeping. I knew also, that he owned more than one car.

What vehicles do you drive?" I asked.

Three cars, two motor-bikes and a Land Rover," he promptly replied.

"That's probably sufficient for the few miles of road on the island. What about putting the money in the bank?" I suggested.

"Why on earth would I do that?" he asked, quite surprised.

"Well, you obviously don't need anything right now, and the money will increase with the interest, and be available when you do need it."

"No, that won't happen. I've got lots more royalties coming in two weeks, so I want to get rid of what I've got before then."

He sold one car, because he was sick of it, and bought a huge American car with a fold-up motorbike in the boot. This naïve attitude in handling money caused the island to go having the richest population per head in the world to being bankrupt in a few short years? In no way do I suggest that this was the fault of the islanders. The fault, I feel, is in those who demanded that they should be given independence, when their experience of life had not prepared them for that responsibility.

The teaching of the island children was a unique and challenging experience. The unexpected happened every day and tested your initiative to find a solution. However, it was a most rewarding experience and one I would hate to have missed. My decision to do it instead of taking up the position of principal of the Melbourne school was thus fully justified.

Some years later, my daughter attended a Melbourne boarding school, where she befriended one of the island girls I had taught. This lass came home with her on weekends and went on a camping holiday with us.

As well as raising a large family, she supervised the training of young teachers on the island.

****

Chapter 10

BACK TO AUSTRALIAN CHILDREN

After that demanding teaching task, I looked forward to something easy at a modern school building in a popular large country town. What I would learn would be that positions in such towns were so desired, that once gained, they were cherished and held for considerable time. The result of this was that teachers often slipped into a rut, with the educating of the children failing to keep up with progress, due to the lack of the injection of the enthusiasm of new blood. A theory that principals should remain in a school no longer than five years was developed for the same reason.

My first day at this school quickly dispelled any thought that I may be in for a more restful time. I was appalled. There was no way I could go along with the dreadful quality of education this large group of children was experiencing. This looked decidedly like the greatest educational challenge I had yet faced, and the preceding experiences could hardly be regarded as a feather bed.

It will take quite a lengthy paragraph to list the problems I noted.

When I arrived the day before school began to set up my room, which was Gr. 6B, I discovered one other teacher doing so too. During our chat, she explained that every grade level had two streams, known far and wide, even by the children, as the bright kids and the dummies. This situation was brought about by the fact that the infant mistress was not just ancient, but had taught at the school almost her entire career. Due to this she knew almost every family, and had in fact taught the parents, and in many cases the grandparents of the present-day children. With this intimate knowledge, she selected from every prep intake, all the children likely to be capable, well behaved pupils, and placed them in the one classroom, which she, of course, taught. All the 'dummies' and likely behaviour problems went into the 'B' stream. This arrangement stayed the same all through the pupils' primary school life, resulting naturally in, that by the time they reached Gr.6, the B stream children had learnt very little other than how to cause trouble.

Being the most recent appointment, thus having no right to any privileged position, I, of course, had been placed in charge of this incorrigible grade. She further informed me that four of the boys had police records, and that the class had sent their Grade 5 teacher off on extended sick leave with a nervous breakdown. Furthermore, four retarded children from the previous year's grade 6, who were far from being competent to go on to secondary school, had been kept back and added to the new Grade six. Some lady teachers were so nervous of them that they would not do yard duty on their own. I could hardly wait to meet this group of monsters.

Having prepared thoroughly the previous day, I used my early arrival on the first day of school to get to know some members of staff and to wander around the grounds a little to gain a feel for the place. Immediately surrounding the school building were two areas, one asphalted and the other a gravel surface. At the back of the school was a huge grassed area, almost the size of a sports oval.

"What a wonderful play area!" I thought, but was surprised to see no children playing on it. They were jammed into the small areas near the school.

"Ah well, anxious to get started," I presumed.

But, to my surprise the situation was the same at morning recess and lunchtime. When class resumed after lunch I questioned the children as to why.

"We aren't allowed to play on the grass," they answered.

I would have to investigate that situation.

To my horror and amazement, reading was still taught throughout the whole school with the old grade readers, a method which had been superseded everywhere else by the use of graded reading schemes and associated activities for some years.

Mathematics was taught still by the old arithmetic style. You may remember that I was involved in the new approach to mathematics. That had been eight years ago. Admittedly the education department could have brought in the change better, but I would be surprised if any other school in the state had not adopted those changes.

The school was almost devoid of audio-visual equipment. The only aid was a Gestetner Stencil printer, but teachers were not permitted to use it, as stencils were too expensive.

It appeared that I was often the only teacher who regular conducted physical education activities and I rarely heard any singing in the upper school.

The place was lifeless, and the attitude of the children reflected this.

To quote my father, 'this was something up with which I could not put'. Being just the fifth most senior member of staff, it might be a difficult task to bring about change, but I had to make the attempt, and in fact, I had to succeed in doing so. It was quite unfair that almost eight hundred children were receiving such a deprived education.

My first priority had to be my own classroom. It was the pits. I managed to see some examples of their work from the previous year. 'Disgusting' was an inadequate word to describe it. Shock treatment seemed necessary.

At the first assembly, I told them to remain in line until the other grades had all gone into school.

"Let's get rid of a bit of holiday rust," I suggested. "Follow me." Heading off at a gentle jog we went all around the school-ground, including the forbidden grassed area. I introduced some hops and jumps and then a few 'funny steps." When they started to puff a little, we stopped for a breather and sat on the ground.

"Did anyone go somewhere special or do something exciting during the holidays?" I asked.

We had a chat for a bit. Someone said, "This is good fun."

When we did go into the classroom, I gave each a piece of paper, and said, "Write about ten lines on the best fun you had in the holidays."

After a while I stopped them.

"You probably have great stories to tell, but sadly I could only read a few of them. I think most of you have a pet spider with ink on its feet and it has walked all over your page. You should all have several exercise books, but you are not going to be allowed to spoil something you are keeping with rubbish like that."

I picked up the only neat page in the class.

"That is nearly satisfactory for a book, but it is the only one in the whole room." That lass, as it happened, had come to us from another school late the previous year. The rest were quite shocked – it was no worse than they had always produced.

Next, I gave them a new sheet of paper, and, step by step, we measured a quarter inch from the edge top and bottom, and carefully, with red pen and ruler made a margin. With great accuracy, we then ruled a red line on the bottom line.

"Start writing next to the margin, but never go over it, and never write on the bottom line," I instructed. "When you begin a lesson, you will print a heading in neat even capital letters, on the top line. Your work won't be crowded, but you won't waste space like some people did last time. Print this heading now."

Everyone does better with specific instructions on which to concentrate. I remember playing on a bowling green next to the skipper of the Australian commonwealth bowls fours and being highly impressed with the instructions he gave his players. Many skippers would say something like,

"Come in on the backhand."

He would say, "You will bowl on the backhand. Come around this short bowl, inside this bowl of ours, and stop right here." Then he would throw his bowls rag on that spot." No doubts remained in the bowler's mind and it surprised me how sometimes quite average bowlers achieved what he demanded.

In this classroom, at this time, I felt that a similar approach was required. Although it did not achieve a miracle, it brought about a remarkable improvement.

To follow up this beginning, I obtained three stamps –unsatisfactory, improved, and very good. When the last of these was earned, that child was sent to the other dummies grades to show what he or she had achieved, and could then pin the page up on the display board. It also earned the right to advance from sheets of paper to working in exercise books.

This may seem a little childish for a Grade 6, but these children had rarely before, if ever, received any form of accolade for what they had done. They glowed with pride at receiving the rewards. My secondary purpose was to improve standards in the other lower dummy grades – I didn't wish to have to repeat this process every year. The teachers of the other grades welcomed this, as it also helped them to raise standards in their classrooms.

In the meantime, all exercise books were to be covered with brown paper or contact and have a favourite picture pasted on the cover. The naming of the book came just prior to use.

A week after school started there came a knock at my classroom door, and in came the principal, escorting two nuns from the catholic school, who, in turn escorted a large red-haired rebellious looking boy. So obvious was the nicotine on his fingers, I immediately noticed that too.

Wasting no time, the senior nun announced loudly that they had brought Jimmy, and were handing him over to my care.

"He has a police record, and we can do nothing with him, so we are hoping you can manage him," she further explained, in a loud voice that all, including the children in my class, could hear.

"What's one more?" I mused to myself. I already had four in my class with police records.

But I was furious – not with the principal for bringing them without warning, and not with Jimmy, but with the nuns who were already publicly making his transition so difficult for him.

"Thank you," I said to them, taking him from them and putting my arm around his shoulder. "We will be very pleased to have you, Jimmy. You may leave him with us and go," I said to the nuns.

"Don't you want to know more about him?" said one surprised nun.

"No thanks, you can tell the principal anything you think necessary. We're keen to get to know Jimmy."

This was almost a repeat of my experience with the itinerant Billy several years ago. Poor Jimmy did not quite know how to react. This was a totally new experience for him. Previously, I guessed, teachers had always been angry with him, and annoyed that they had him in their class. I introduced him to the class and found him a seat. His rebellious expression disappeared, replaced first by puzzlement, and soon followed by a tentative smile

From that day, Jimmy gave me no trouble. He was happy. Academically he was a problem, of course, but otherwise he was fine.

As an element of my philosophy insisted, *it is important to love your pupils and make that fact obvious to them.*

He, along with the rest of the class gradually began to develop some self-pride and self-confidence.

At the first staff conference, I raised the subject of the children being forbidden to play on the grassed area. Addressing the principal, I said, "All the seven hundred children are crowded into a small playing area. Why can't they play on the grass?"

"Because it is too long and they could get grass seeds in their socks. There is also the possibility of snakes," he explained.

"The best thing to do with long grass is to mow it. All would then be solved," I suggested.

"Not even to be considered – too expensive," he adamantly stated.

Like a dog with a bone I persevered.

"If the grass were short they could play there then?" I asked.

"Of course!" he snorted. "But it's not going to happen."

"I wouldn't bet on that," I mused, but kept it to myself.

That was Wednesday after school. The following day, rather unusually, I left early after school along with most of the teachers, but I was on a mission. With two large bottles of beer in my possession I drove off in search of the council mower. Before long I located it and approached its operator.

After a short chat, we had become like old friends. To my delight, he listened to my predicament and was disgusted that the children were deprived of the playing area.

"I can't pay you, but it would be worth these two bottles to you, if you could sneak in after work and mow it," I offered with a bit of a grin.

After accepting the two bottles it was his turn to grin.

"You've just wasted your money," he chuckled. "I would have done it for nothing. It's a ridiculous situation. I knock off a bit early tomorrow and the school is on my way home. You can consider the grass mown."

"Thanks," I responded. "But it's money well spent rather than wasted by my reckoning."

"You can forget the problem," he assured me, and, as an after-thought, added. "Just make sure that double gate is unlocked and it will be mown every second Friday."

Bribe

We departed, friends, and both well satisfied.

On the Monday morning, I arrived early and directed the children down to the grass, where they ran freely, chasing each other delightedly. The staff members were not so thrilled, as now an extra teacher would need to be on yard duty to patrol the larger area. They began to get the feeling that perhaps I could prove to be a problem.

By the following staff meeting I had formed my tactics for approaching the shortcomings of the course of study. The physical education seemed the easiest and quickest to solve. Teachers found excuses not to conduct Phys. Ed., mainly weather. It was too hot or too cold, too windy or too wet.

At the meeting, I offered to co-ordinate sport and physical education, which included organising inter-house sport and inter-school sport, and planning and writing the physical education course.

Everyone jumped at the offer as it freed them from maybe being given the task.

For physical education, I planned a program that involved a team effort of four classes, with the four teachers each being responsible for a group. The groups rotated from each activity to the next. One group did game skills, another exercises and gymnastics, yet another did dance, and the fourth a games session. A four-week program was set out and it changed every month. As each teacher was part of a team, nobody could opt out at the last minute on some conjured up pretext. At first, they were reluctant, but it was so successful, and the children gained so much pleasure and benefit, that, before long, the teachers too, became enthused.

Win number two.

It was time to tackle number three.

I decided on maths. Sneakily, I didn't suggest that we adopt the new maths and demanded nothing, as the principal's automatic reaction to a request or demand was a reflex *no*. He was morbidly afraid that it might cost money, or ruffle the peaceful waters.

Instead, I approached him in his office one day, and said, "I have a set of multi attribute blocks. Perhaps you would like me to demonstrate to the staff how they are used for a few minutes each staff meeting." Most teachers are petrified of the dreaded district inspector and are desperate to impress him. The principal was distinctly of this school of thought, so I cunningly added, "I have known the new inspector for a long time, and I know he is very enthusiastic about the new maths course." I was a firm believer that a white lie for a good cause was justified.

Feeling safe, as there seemed to be no money involved, he agreed. After a few weeks, the teachers began to understand the course, asked many questions, and I began to see light at the end of the tunnel. Choosing my time carefully, I again casually brought up the inspector's enthusiasm for the course, and before long many were converted to the cause. Although the principal eventually grudgingly finally agreed to dip into his well-guarded funds, we started, on the bare minimum materials needed for the course, and had to use our initiative and ingenuity to supplement them.

Win number three.

My next target obviously had to be reading. This I had left until last, as it was by far the most expensive, as well as being a widely different technique. Any change caused fear and trembling, so this would be quite a shock, and should be well planned before hitting them with it.

In the meantime, I gradually broached the subject of singing. I conducted lots of singing throughout most days, but rarely did I hear singing anywhere else throughout the upper school, that is Grades 3-6. After much quiet investigation, all teachers except two really felt they could teach singing, but just didn't get around to doing much of it.

Eventually, most conceded that they should and would in future. Of the two who claimed to be tone deaf and not game to do it, one had quite a flair for teaching art. He agreed to take my grade for a double art lesson each week, so I was freed to teach his and the grade of the other teacher who felt unable to take singing. The latter and I alternated between the two grades. Everyone was happy with this arrangement, particularly the children.

Good naturedly, the teachers complained about me totally wrecking the calm, relaxed status quo, but, by the start of term three I felt it was time to tackle the reading. Obviously, the biggest hurdle would be the principal, as it was an expensive business to begin it. Knowing his money-spending phobia, and having already raided his bank account for maths equipment, I approached it by a roundabout route.

"You'd probably like to start on the new approach to reading to keep up with other schools, but we wouldn't have the funds required," I said during an amicable conversation.

"You're right there," he agreed. "But it's most unlike you to think of conserving money," he added with suspicion and wariness in his voice.

"Right," I agreed. "Of course, it wouldn't be a problem if we managed to raise the necessary amount of money."

"You are dreaming!" he snorted. "Our only money source is the Mothers' Club and they have nothing like that."

"My idea was a combined money raising effort by the mothers, the school committee and the teachers. I even think I could get support from my Apex Club if they understood the need."

"No way!" he said. "I wouldn't even think of asking them."

"Actually, I was thinking of doing the asking. Would you be agreeable to me addressing the various groups?" I asked.

"You'd be butting your head against a brick wall," he assured me. "I can't really stop you, but I'll assure them that I didn't put you up to it."

Contrary to his expectations, after I had explained how far our methods were behind, all the groups previously mentioned were so enthusiastic they could hardly wait to start. I suggested a large fair at the school on a Saturday and offered to co-ordinate these diverse groups. Aided by that diversity, it was surprising how many contacts they had between them, and we ran an amazingly successful fair, with all sorts of rides, stalls, competitions and games. The children in senior grades, made eye-catching posters, that were prominently displayed around both our town and surrounding towns. To our delight the money raised was beyond our wildest dreams, and we not only set the school up for a successful reading program, but were able to upgrade our maths equipment and materials. It even brought a smile to our principal's face, as there was some left over for him to sit on and guard.

Teachers who were trained under the two-year college course were qualified for lower levels on the promotion chain, but had to do extra studies in the form of vacation schools and a year of practical teaching of each subject studied to progress further. The teaching year had to be approved by an inspector. I had completed all subjects to reach the top of the profession, except the practical teaching of horticulture. Always interested in improved methods of teaching, as indicated by my original involvement in the introduction of new maths, the imminent arrival of a science course to replace the rather limited nature study subject interested me. I had planned to write a possible course, and teach it a year in advance of its official introduction. When I mentioned this to the inspector near the beginning of my first year there, he was most enthusiastic. I explained that if I taught the year of horticulture I could not fit in both. He suggested that I do the science, and include three or four lessons of a horticultural nature in it, and he would pass me.

This I did, and toward the end of the year I requested an inspection to approve my horticulture.

"But you have taught science, not horticulture. I can't possibly pass that as horticulture," was his response to my request.

I could not believe my ears – it had even been his idea. It would not be proper to write what I called him. Teachers can't speak to inspectors in such a manner, and our rather tenuous friendship ended abruptly, cancelled permanently by both parties.

All went well the following year, and a considerable degree of improvement in both pupil enthusiasm and performance took place.

One interesting incident occurred. During a year in a one-teacher school nearby, followed by a year as infant mistress in another school in the town, Elaine had proved what a competent teacher she was. Our children attended the third large school in town. At the age of eleven, Kerrie was tested, and was found to have a reading age of sixteen, and Doug, aged nine, achieved a reading age of fourteen. Their teachers were most impressed, and invited us to the school to explain what wonderful methods we had used to teach reading to our children.

"When Kerrie was four, she suffered bronchial asthma and pneumonia. The doctor suggested she be moved from Melbourne to a warmer climate for a while, so she went to stay with her grandparents in the Mallee," I explained to them.

I imagine they must have wondered where this was all leading.

"She drove her grandfather mad wanting him to read her stories in the manner she was accustomed to at home. Driven to distraction, he borrowed a John and Betty prep grade reader from the local school. 'Kerrie, it's time you learnt to read. Watch,' he demanded, and pointed to the words as he read, 'This is John. This is Betty, and so on.

Before long she moved on to the readers of grade 1 and 2. She was there for just over three weeks and arrived home able to read. Soon she severely said to her young brother, "Douglas, it's time you learnt to read. Watch while I point. This is John. This is Betty."

Young Doug was reading by the time he turned three. I'm afraid their clever teacher parents can claim no credit, and no wondrous teaching method was employed. We just stood by and watched the magic happen."

I'm sure the teachers must have been disappointed, their hopes of learning the secret to brilliant teaching of reading dashed.

"What we did do," I added, as some explanation, "was read to them often from their cradle days, and I always made up a serial bedtime story for each, so we did encourage their love of reading. They always had books."

Early in the second year, my principal called me to the office.

Don," he said, "you must apply for an annual inspection. Without doubt you have earned an advanced promotion assessment."

"Not a chance," I scoffed. "The inspector and I are on most unfriendly terms."

"I will support your cause," he insisted. "I won't accept a *no*."

So I applied. The inspector left the inspection until the second last week of the year. He did not award the mark I needed."

If a teacher feels unjustly treated, he can appeal, and if his appeal is accepted he can receive an inspection from another inspector. I sent in a most convincing appeal, but, as I left the district at the end of that year, there was no chance of another inspection, and the case was automatically dropped. However, at my next school, even before I had a chance to prove myself, the inspector suggested he inspect my work, and awarded the advanced promotion assessment.

A fun thing occurred at a function to farewell me from the school where I had bullied the staff into change. One of the older teachers wrote a short story and read it. It went as follows :- 'Once there was a forest. Nothing ever disturbed its peaceful calm. The trees swayed slightly to and fro in the gentlest of breezes that always prevailed, and the whole forest sighed contentedly. Suddenly the peace was shattered by the arrival of a terrible storm. The trees of the forest bent low to the ground and almost broke before its irresistible force. It paused over the forest for some time causing dreadful havoc. As always with storms, however, it eventually passed, and with a grateful sigh, the trees prepared to settle back into their previous calm, peaceful existence.'

It was very cleverly written and its significance was lost on nobody, particularly me. I rose to respond.

"If you even consider that, be assured I'll return in spirit and haunt you mercilessly." I threatened.

There was much laughing response, but I am confident that the threat was never carried out. Most of them seemed to really enjoy their altered, up to date approach.

****

Chapter 11

REST AT LAST

During my second year at the previous school, my friend, 'Wistle' had arrived for a weekend visit. He had gained a position at a consolidated school. For the uninitiated, in some farming areas, several small schools close down and the children are bussed to a new large school, known as a consolidated school. These schools were usually in a modern, well-equipped building, set in extensive surrounds. They were an experiment that the education department was anxious to succeed, and as such, received rather special treatment and privileges.

"A position in charge of the middle school is becoming vacant at the school," he announced." I'm sure you could get it. It's a dream posting, and it would be great for us to work together again,"

This suggestion sounded very tempting.

I was interested, particularly when he continued, gilding the proposition.

"The vice principal is the infant mistress, fully occupied in the infant department. We rarely see the principal unless we visit the office, in which he sits all day dreaming up ideas. Officially I am in charge only of Grades 5 & 6, but, in actual fact, the boss virtually leaves the day to day running of the school to me. Other than during our second year on Nauru, the staff is by far the best I've known. If you fill my role in the middle department, together we would make it the best school in the state. Am I tempting you?"

"More than that. You've dangled the juiciest carrot I have been offered. I'm on my way."

After the enormous effort I had put into righting the wrongs where I was, I needed a more restful situation. This was obviously just that.

I managed to get appointed to the position and found that 'Wistle had not exaggerated the qualities of the school. As well as the two of us there were four outstanding men teachers on the staff – outstanding teaching ability, outgoing fun personalities and highly motivated. It was easy to build an excellent team around such a nucleus. Furthermore, the whole staff was happy, and much fun was created by them, both in the confines of the staffroom and when amongst the children. The result was that the same attitude rubbed off on the children, who were fun to teach. It seemed I was in educational heaven – classrooms well equipped, a school librarian, and an art and craft specialist in an exciting separate room. Outside of the school building, we had a large oval and almost exclusive use of the town oval, which adjoined it. To finally gild the lily, the town swimming pool fence began perhaps fifteen yards beyond one corner of the school-ground. As we were the only school to use it, swimming lessons could take place every day in the short summer period. I regard learning to swim well to be as important as the basic subjects.

For the first time, I was in a position to indulge in my belief that taking children away on a camp gave them a most valuable experience. In this camping environment, they developed initiative, independence, responsibility and a wonderful rapport with the teacher camp leaders. I would take at least one other teacher and some very carefully selected parents as leaders. To go away on camp in the first month of the year was an invaluable beginning to the year by everyone who attended. The children would be given responsibilities, including kitchen duties, waiting on tables, and keeping their sleeping quarters and the whole campsite clean and tidy. The responsibility of setting up activities like an obstacle course and a flying fox would also be theirs, closely supervised, of course by leaders. They would take part in a wide range of activities including tackling the obstacle course, studying nature and learning bushcraft, hikes, including a pre-dawn hike to a suitable site to watch the sunrise, handcrafts, games, and preparing and performing a concert item.

Flying Fox at Camp

My title would be 'BIG CHIEF', and I would answer only to that. Other leaders would be named Chief Something or Other, and the children would be braves or squaws and divided into tribes. The week would be highly competitive, with various ways to earn points. Certificates of competence were awarded for several activities, making sure all children received some, but they had to reach a standard, and were often not awarded at the first attempt. They loved the chance to address me as Big Chief instead of Mr Roberts. That title of course ended when camp finished, and interestingly that privilege was never abused.

The ongoing benefits of that week were considerable, both in the children's personalities and self-confidence, and in the rapport between pupils and teachers.

As 'Wistle predicted, the principal left the organising of the upper school to the two of us, and as he further predicted, the school developed into, if not the best in the state, then certainly we matched the best. This really didn't necessarily reflect great credit on the two of us. The enthusiasm and quality of the staff as a whole, produced the result. The two years spent at this school would rank at the top of my enjoyable years of teaching, without too much effort by me, and with practically no pressure or stress.

****

Chapter 12

NO CLASSROOM

All good things come to an end – sometimes earlier than we would wish. After two blissful years, I gained promotion to a Class 1 vice principal position at a school in the Wimmera District of Victoria.

The day before school started, I sat chatting with George, my new principal. As he had passed sixty, and many principals are winding down to retirement by then, I was pleased to see that he was still interested in his school performing well.

Although lacking a little in imagination and progressive thinking, he was doing a solid job, and proved open to suggestion and change.

"Quite remarkably we have an extra member of staff, Don, a girl fresh out of teachers' college. What do you suggest we do with her?"

"Give her a class. She would be mortified if she didn't get a chance to have her own group, and without experience, would prove to be lost and rather useless as an extra," I said with conviction.

"Well, who doesn't have a classroom?"

"Me, of course," I responded, already making plans.

"But I can handle the office on my own. What on earth would you do?"

"How much time do you have?" I said with a smile.

'Hit me with it." He settled back in his chair.

"To begin with, I would supervise and assist teachers in writing the course of study for the year and their weekly work programs. I'll make sure all teachers have a complete and imaginative program to follow."

"Sounds like a good start," he approved. "What then?"

"Next I would suggest that I test the whole school on the basics, specifically reading and maths. I suspect that around ten per cent will have problems in one or the other, perhaps even more than that." It would be a shame if that many progressed to secondary school so ill prepared, and that is happening in many districts. I had deliberately said *suggest*, as I really didn't want him to feel I was pushing too hard, or trying to take decision making over. That definitely had to remain his prerogative.

"What would you do when you come up with the results?" he asked curiously.

"I would like to conduct a remedial program, preferably with about six children coming to me at a time, so it could be very individual."

"You are really beginning to interest me," he said, leaning forward. "This could work out very well."

"I also have another angle in mind," I continued. "Grade 6 children benefit enormously from going on a camp early in their final primary school year. And we all know that if you have an outstanding grade 6, it follows that you develop a really good school."

"No teachers on staff and none of the children have any experience of school camping." There was doubt in his voice.

"I have," I assured him. "I would plan the week thoroughly, okay it with you and the children's parents, and I will lead the camp myself."

'It certainly should have advantages," he said, thinking aloud.

"Sleepovers at the school for lower grades are a great preparation for a camp when reaching Grade 6," I added.

"One more matter. A remedial program like I propose costs money. Suitable reading material for all ages is a must, and you also need plenty of concrete materials for the maths, particularly multi-attribute blocks. We would need the support of the mothers' club and school committee."

That's where I can contribute," he sounded enthusiastic. "You may need to address them and explain your plans, but I'm sure I can enthuse them,"

It seemed George and I might form an effective team.

"You will also find that with Elaine in charge of the library, it will become the hub around which the school revolves, which is exciting," I predicted, knowing well that would be the case.

"That will be most welcome, too," he assured me.

"One more thing I am really set on," I concluded. "Happy children learn best, so no child should experience things like school-ground bullying. I'd like to organise a happy school-ground program, which would include a buddy system and a strong teacher presence in the school grounds at recess and lunch breaks."

"I hope you can convince the staff, but I'm happy to support that. I can hardly wait for school to start."

The testing of the school from Grade 2 upwards, uncovered 37 almost total non-readers and almost as many with a severe maths weakness. The majority of these children were in the higher grades, so there was no time to waste if they were to be ready to progress to the secondary school.

"That's an enormous number, "said George, most concerned. "I would never have thought it would be so high."

"It is," I agreed. "But many of those children will have fallen behind due to an absence, or because the program progressed too fast for them to keep pace, causing them to give up because they couldn't catch up. By the end of the year that number should reduce considerably. It did prove a little expensive to run the remedial program, as I checked out the interests of each child and purchased books of suitable difficulty on all those topics. As is claimed, however, the proof of the pudding is in the eating. From the parent groups down, we all agreed that the expense, and all the effort, proved to be worthwhile, when thirty-two of the thirty-seven children became competent readers by the end of the year. The other five would probably always have reading difficulties, but did show improvement. Probably the most rewarding factor for me was the blossoming of their personalities as the year progressed. It was living proof of my theory that every child should be convinced that he or she is capable in at least one area.

In most cases the inability to understand maths had stemmed from getting behind at some stage and never being able to catch up. This may have been due to an absence, or the program moving too fast. I would need to spend time in classrooms during maths lessons to make sure it wasn't the latter. It proved easier to resolve the maths weaknesses than the reading problem. By the end of that year, and in some cases, much earlier, almost all the remedial group had a satisfactory grasp on maths.

The camp, held at a permanent campsite in the Grampian Mountains, was thoroughly enjoyed by children and leaders alike, and produced the desired changes in the children's behaviour and attitude. I took on the title of Big Chief again, and answered to nothing else. The procedure followed the same lines as described in the previous chapter and the resulting effect on the children was hugely satisfying

All the children developed independence, self-confidence and initiative through shared activities attempted, and an excellent rapport developed between the teachers and the children.

Bullying became almost non-existent, due to the policy on ground supervision plus the buddy system.

During the previous year, our last year at the consolidated school, we left the school soon after three-thirty to have a cup of tea at home, before returning to the school. Despite our early arrival, we were most surprised to find that our two children, who attended the high school fourteen miles away, had arrived home before us.

"How come you are here?" I asked.

The answer I received was the final straw that broke the camel's back. It added to my annoyance that, at a recent parent teacher interview, the teachers could not comment on my children without looking it all up. Being so ill-informed clearly contravened my belief in being really interested in each child you teach. I not only knew the name, and all about every child in my grade, but most of the other children throughout the school. The answer from my children to my question on this present occasion infuriated me.

"The teachers decided to go on strike at lunch time and didn't let the buses know, so we had to find a way home ourselves."

They were twelve and thirteen years old.

"You mean you had to hitchhike along that highway?" I almost shouted.

Whatever the cost we were sending them away to a school of our choosing the following year.

This, however, resulted in them having to arrive home at 2.30am on Saturday and leave at 2.30am on Monday. Despite them loving their weekends at the rambling old farmhouse we rented, this situation had to change. Elaine could move as her position was not permanent, but I was stuck for three years. The only chance of moving was to be seconded to a position outside the education department. A few years earlier I had been offered the job of vice principal at the Victorian Police Academy, but had knocked it back, as I had no wish to return to Melbourne at the time. Contacting the academy, I discovered that the position had again become vacant and it was again offered to me. Elaine gained a position of head teacher of a small two-teacher school with a residence within commuting distance of Melbourne, and I would commute to work daily with a friend who already did so – problem solved.

In late November, the Director of Primary Education suddenly decided that he would cease seconding senior teachers to anywhere, and my secondment was summarily cancelled.

For twelve months, Elaine and I lived apart, except for weekends, forcing me to travel 160 miles each way each weekend. Doug lived with Elaine, and Kerrie boarded in Melbourne, coming home when she could. This arrangement had to change.

An interesting situation arose at the start of that extraordinary year. A visitor arrived at the school and the message delivered to me by a child said that the police wanted to see me. Now the one and only policeman in town was a young man, whom I had taught some years ago in a Grade 4.

"Don," he greeted me, "the bush telegraph informs me that you will be living on your own for this year."

"As usual, John, the bush telegraph is on the ball," I assured him.

"Well, unless you have better arrangements, you must come and live with me. I have two bedrooms going to waste and you would be very welcome to fill one."

"A rather unusual scenario," I thought, "a teacher and an ex-pupil living as housemates." But I was very chuffed that he would be prepared to make such an offer.

Aloud I said, "I can't imagine a better arrangement. When can I move in?"

"Today or earlier would be fine," he settled with a satisfied grin.

We developed a most affable relationship, with him taking great pleasure in introducing me to his mates, even to the extent of waking me at any time during the night with,

"Hey, Robbo. Wake up.

Come in fellas and have a drink with my teacher mate, Robbo."

Never, at 3.00 am, or there about, did I ever feel like a drink with a group of young blokes who had already over-imbibed. However, I never refused.

****

CHAPTER 13

THE TOUGHEST TEST OF ALL

After seeking a compassionate transfer unsuccessfully, I demoted to take up a Class 2 principal position in a school of just over two hundred pupils. I had no illusions that this would be easy. A Class 2 principal was, in fact, the most demanding position in the state at that time. You were the principal, and had all the responsibilities that principals of the largest schools have, but none of the help. No secretary was appointed to help run the office, and I was quite often required to do some classroom teaching.

Arriving at the school in mid-January to 'case the joint', I suddenly stopped in my tracks, hardly able to believe my eyes. I saw an average modern style school building set on a steep hill. It was not the school itself that demanded my attention, but what was written in large white painted letters across every window. Again, and again, I read 'JOHNSON IS A WEAK BASTARD.' Johnson was the name of my predecessor. What sort of children attended this school? I firmly vowed that they would never have that opinion of me.

My first reaction was to investigate a little – prior knowledge could be very handy. Before long I had a fair idea of the situation I faced. The children from a home for deserted and disturbed boys all attended the school. They were difficult, as many, if not all, had serious emotional problems. However, I was reliably informed that they were by no means my most difficult pupils. Many local children were far worse, the girls quite as bad as the boys. An almost unbelievable scenario unfolded. Apparently, the whole school was banned from participating in any inter-school event, as they invariably wrecked the day. The local bus line refused to allow them on their buses, as they always wrecked the bus in which they travelled. The teachers were wary of the children and emergency teachers refused to act as replacements, particularly in the infamous grade 6.

My policy when beginning at a new school or new grade had always been to be friendly but firm, beginning with the friendly, but being firm at the first sign of misbehaviour, and then being consistent about what was and was not acceptable. Children loved the friendliness, but also appreciated knowing exactly where they stood.

After much consideration, I decided that, in this situation, I had better reverse the order. Firm would come first, followed by the friendliness when that was deserved.

On the very first morning this resolve was thoroughly tested.

Unfortunately, I was totally preoccupied in the office before school began. Glued to the phone I began to hear the loud noise of what sounded like many children inside the school building. While still bound to the phone, I heard one very loud voice swearing quite violently. As soon as I could end the phone call I charged into the corridor, to be surrounded by a horde of children and one lady teacher.

"Did you hear that boy shouting swear words?" I addressed her.

"Certainly," she admitted.

I resisted asking why she had not dealt with the situation.

Instead I asked, "Who was he swearing at in such a vile manner?"

"At me," she admitted.

I was amazed that she appeared to think little of it.

"Has it happened before?" I asked.

"Oh, it's a common occurrence. It happens all the time."

"Change that to 'It used to happen all the time,'" I gritted, then added, "Would you come into the office for a few minutes, please?"

I sooled all the children off outside and followed her into the office and closed the door. Firstly, I apologised for not introducing myself earlier and learned her name. I then plied her with questions and learned much more, none of it being good news. During the days preceding school, I had met my new second-in-charge. Interestingly she had received the compassionate transfer that I had been denied, as her husband had moved for his job.

And they say it's a man's world.

I had met one or two other teachers, who had come to spend some time preparing their room, but those conversations had been brief, mainly just getting-to-know sessions, rather talking shop.

Questioning her, I gathered that almost all the staff consisted of young ladies, several being quite inexperienced. There were two male teachers - I would have preferred more, but if the two were strong, they could be of great value. They were not strong, and of very little value, as I lost one after a few weeks, and the other in early April, both to sick leave due to nervous breakdowns. Their leave was for the whole year.

Before she left the office, I arranged for her to inconspicuously point out the miscreant who had sworn at her, when the children lined up at assembly.

Armed with this information, I addressed the assembly in a no-nonsense authoritative voice, which fortunately I possessed

"In the short time I have been here, I have heard many shocking reports about the behaviour of children of this school. Those reports make me very angry. I will not hear them again, because that type of behaviour has stopped as of this minute. Any child who behaves badly will come directly to me, and will wish he or she had never had to do so - just as one boy will feel in a few minutes." I paused for that to sink in.

"While on the phone this morning, I heard shouted swearing in the corridor. It was a boy swearing at a teacher. I could not believe my ears. This does not happen in a school, and certainly it will never again happen in this school. I did not see this boy at the time as I was too busy on the phone, but I will find him if I need to. Hopefully that will not be necessary. He has one chance to own up, and come out here on the steps with me, apologise to that teacher in front of the whole school, and promise that it won't ever happen again. If he has the courage to do that his punishment will be less. If he doesn't, I will find him and his punishment will be very severe. That boy has ten seconds to come forward."

At the end of the ten seconds nobody had moved.

"All right. You have had your chance," I said.

"Now, you will all stand to attention and look straight into my eyes as I walk slowly along the lines."

Starting with the back line so it didn't drag out too long, I soon stopped at the guilty boy. Even without previous knowledge, I would have had no doubts about who was guilty. He was having great difficulty maintaining eye contact with me.

I smiled at him and stated, "Well, I didn't have to go far, did I."

Taking him by the arm I led him to the top step in front of the assembly, so all the children, who all looked a little stunned by the process, could see him.

To make sure he could not become a hero with smug grins, I warned him.

"By the way, the first smart look or grin on your face will further increase your punishment, and you are not going to enjoy that punishment, as it is."

He looked very sheepish and self-conscious throughout the Monday morning ceremony.

Before the ceremony, I softened the blow a little.

"I know some of you have not behaved badly in the past and I congratulate you children who have behaved well when those around you have not been doing so. Everyone will behave like you this year."

After the saluting of the flag and reciting the pledge, I explained what was to follow. Apparently, they had previously wandered into school when it suited them before the siren signalled the time for school to begin. After recesses and lunch breaks, they straggled in, taking as long as the mood moved them.

"From now on, children will only enter the school building before school starts on the invitation of a teacher. We will always assemble and march to our rooms before school, and as recess times and lunchtimes end. Infant grades will lead off with senior school classes following. Today, however, you will march around the quadrangle first to show me that you can march well."

Addressing my miscreant, I said, "Now, you can re-join your class to learn to march, but you will stop off at my office as your class passes it." As they marched I gave a good imitation of a tough sergeant major, insisting on straight backs and keeping in step.

As expected, my villain was from the infamous Grade 6, which suited me, as they would be my first and main target. As he entered the classroom after leaving my office, he performed an excellent act of wringing what were no doubt stinging hands. Striking while the iron was hot, I asked the teacher if he would man the office while I took his grade. My approach was quite different from that used at assembly, explaining to them their importance to the school due to the influence they had as the oldest kids. As such, they were automatically role models and mimicked by the rest of the school. In this way, I actually gave them responsibility, and enlisted their help and co-operation in turning the school's reputation around. I deliberately didn't mention the fact that they had been the main instigators of that reputation.

Another responsibility I offered them was becoming music master or mistress. The school had a blaring siren to signal school starting, recess and lunch beginning and ending and the end of the school day. I had only heard it once, but t6hat was enough. I hated it. It jarred my senses, made me feel irritated, almost aggro. It occurred to me that if it had this effect on me, it quite probably had a similar effect on the children. I had always loved music and was a firm believer in what I termed the magic of music and the effect it had on the emotions. That siren had to go. In its place, I decided to play music, beginning softly for about fifteen seconds and gradually increasing in volume, but never becoming loud. I arranged for a teacher to start it one morning so that I could watch its effect firsthand. The effect on the children was quite remarkable. Surprise showed on their faces, quickly followed by smiles. When they realised what it meant, they moved off without any of the usual running around, arguing, and sometimes annoying each other. A few even adjusted their steps to the rhythm of the music. As time went by, I varied the music played. Every teacher, several children, and even some neighbours commented approvingly, and the Gr.6 children vied for the privilege of the responsibility. I feel it played a major part in changing the behaviour pattern of the whole school, and the Gr. 6 children in particular.

Angels, the latter did not become, in fact they sent their teacher off with a nervous breakdown in early April. Leopards don't change their spots overnight, but it was a start and some did respond. The departure of their teacher with his nervous breakdown brought both disadvantages and benefits. My load was greatly increased, as no emergency teacher would come to the school to take that grade, labelling them incorrigible and impossible to handle. The advantage was that I had to teach them, and thus had the chance to modify their behaviour. By using a reward system, I achieved some instant improvement. As a school phone rarely stops ringing, I needed a responsible child to be in the office and answer it. They competed for the right to be head teacher. The best-behaved children, who had worked diligently, were rewarded by becoming the phone monitor at the office. They also soon became interested in earning points for their house, an activity I featured.

As the only other man on the staff had also left even before the grade 6 teacher, and remained on sick leave due to nerves for the remainder of the year, I was left as the only man with a staff consisting of lady teachers, some of whom, would not perform yard duty on their own. They insisted on me, preferably, or at least, another teacher accompanying them.

After school on the second day of the year, I held the first staff conference, at which I explained my aims.

"I'm sure you haven't enjoyed working in the atmosphere that has prevailed here in the past, and I'm equally sure you wish to improve it. I have formulated a definite plan of action, which I know will achieve that purpose with your co-operation. Any input you have to offer I will be most happy to incorporate into that plan."

Introducing my plan, I went on to state that the best procedure was not through punishment of bad behaviour when it occurred, although blatant misbehaviour would be punished, and we needed to be consistent with that. The better course by far was to prevent the wrong-doing by making school so interesting and so much fun that the children would have no desire to misbehave.

Considerable emphasis should be placed on activities they would enjoy, such as physical education, competitive activities, singing and acting. Reward and demerit points should be extensively awarded for the house system, which already existed, but had received little consideration.

Effective preparation is paramount to effective teaching, and this begins with your yearly courses of study. I have read them carefully and I am afraid I am not impressed. We need to revise them, and this I would like us to do together. Social studies is well covered, the reading and English courses, although needing attention are fairly complete, maths is very skimpy and the recently introduced science subject is distinctly vague, varying little from the old nature study. With your agreement, I would like to complete the physical education and music programs first, as I want them to feature early. When they are completed we need to tackle the maths and science. After we are satisfied with those subjects we will work on the reading and English courses. It will obviously take the whole year, as I have no wish to make the task too onerous."

To my great satisfaction, this speech met with enthusiastic responses of agreement and promises of co-operation.

Unfortunately, it also provided the first spark that ignited what would develop into an ongoing war between the district inspector and me. The inspector was a domineering personality who thrust his face well into your personal space as he made his dogmatic demands. The scene was inevitably set for a clash of personalities between us.

After introducing himself on his first visit to the school, he wasted no time in announcing his mission.

"I intend writing a thesis on the teaching of English in primary schools this year," he announced in a voice that reverberated around my office. "The material for this will be derived from detailed courses of study, consisting of an absolute minimum of six typed foolscap sheets, from every school in my inspectorate. I expect thorough research and minute detail on content and method of teaching. You will begin immediately, and have it to me before the end of term one." It was obviously a decree not to be questioned.

My response left him incredulous, mouth open in total disbelief, as normally all teachers obey a district inspector without question, particularly him.

"I commend your project, and am sure it will fill a need. But I'm afraid my school won't be able to participate unless you are prepared to wait until close to the end of the year."

For just one moment his mouth opened and closed like a fish out of water.

"Correct me if I am wrong," he eventually viciously spat out, spacing his words for maximum impact. "That sounds as if you are defying an order from me, your inspector."

"You are quite correct in your assumption," I assured him. "But I will explain and I'm sure that you, as an educator yourself, will understand and concur with my reasons. As you must surely know, having inspected this school last year, our school has some serious problems. We, the staff and I, are tackling these problems in order of severity and urgency of need, and already have a detailed plan. English comes well down the order of need."

"I'll pretend I have not heard this, and will expect you to, after some time to think, see the wisdom of reversing your response." he threateningly stated.

As he was turning to leave in a huff, I finished the confrontation with,

"There cannot be a reversal, as a principal's first responsibility is to the children and staff of his school, not to the desires of an inspector or anyone else."

Due to the fact that the inspector is the final authority, and also controls the future careers of teachers, I had committed an unwise crime, and expected that he would make my life difficult, which in fact he did. However, I could not, and did not, veer from what I believed.

Before long I had managed to reverse the ban placed by the bus line on my school. There was, however, one condition, which I offered, and to which they dubiously finally agreed. No bus would transport any of our children unless I, personally, rode with them to guarantee behaviour. I had even given them a detailed list of suggested behavioural expectations, of which they approved.

One day, a young lady whom I regarded very highly as a teacher, came to my office in tears. She taught a Grade 2, usually regarded as consisting of delightful children, still affectionate, but having left behind their baby ways and being a little more independent.

"I am going to have to resign from teaching," she sobbed. "I am totally inadequate as a teacher, and can do nothing with Malcolm. He comes into school after a recess with many stones in his shirt, which is rolled up in front of him, and proceeds to throw them at me and other children. He even tips over tables and threatens to hit me with a chair. It is totally unfair on the other children."

Armed and Ready

"I agree with your conclusion but strongly disagree with your admission of inadequacy. In fact, you are one of the best young teachers I have ever known. You must continue to teach, but I will take Malcolm until I decide what to do with him."

Butter wouldn't have melted in Malcolm's mouth when he was with me in the office, but of course that arrangement could not continue for long. Contacting the boys' home immediately shed light on the situation. His mother had deserted him, dumping him at the home. After some time, they found a foster home for him and he was happy. As sometimes happens when a child is in the home, his foster mother finally managed to become pregnant. No longer wanting Malcolm, she returned him to the home. He thus learned to hate women in the age group of his two ex-mothers, which was about the age group of his teacher, so he took out his anger on her.

What to do? I found that in the nearest school to ours there was a lovely grandmotherly lady teaching the grade 2. Contacting both her and her principal, I explained our predicament with Malcolm.

"The poor little lamb," was her immediate response. "He must come to my classroom as soon as you can arrange it."

Herein lay the problem. The district inspector, who was away for the following fortnight at a conference, is supposed to give his approval before an action like this is taken. I decided the matter was too important and urgent to wait for him, and I was not entirely confident that he would approve the change anyway.

The plan was a raging success. His new teacher and her class welcomed Malcolm without the slightest hitch. He immediately loved her and his new situation, and was happy.

On the day the inspector returned, I informed him of what we had arranged and why. He almost went purple in the face with anger.

"Rules and the correct procedure mean nothing to you, do they," he raged.

"Not when a child's welfare and a fine young teacher's future are at urgent risk, no. Presuming you would hold the welfare of all those concerned as paramount, I felt you would approve."

"You felt wrong. It could have waited," he concluded. However, it was too late to change it again, so all finished well, except that the relationship between him and me deteriorated even further.

That relationship became even worse when he arrived to inspect the school during morning recess one day. A young lad had just been brought to me with a broken icy-pole stick struck firmly in his throat. Having already tried unsuccessfully to remove it, I knew that it was stuck fast and was going nowhere without treatment from a doctor. I had rung the hospital to inform them that I was on my way. They approved my decision and were waiting at the ready.

Enter the inspector.

"You can't drive him," he insisted. "You must ring an ambulance."

I had no intention of wasting further time arguing with him, except to say that the lad was most uncomfortable and quite distressed, and that I would be at the hospital before an ambulance could even arrive at the school. So saying, I drove off with another teacher sitting with the boy to comfort him and keep him calm. Of course, everything went according to plan.

Returning to the school I was greeted by a lady teacher in great distress. She was very pregnant and suffered the emotional fragility that sometimes accompanies that state. She was overdue to take leave to have the baby. Her teaching I could in no way fault - she was brilliant, making her Grade 3 program really exciting to the children, while her teaching of the basic subjects was very sound. Under that prevailing situation, I ignored the fact that her weekly work program resembled a battleground of warring spiders with their feet covered in ink.

"He showed not a shred of interest in the work I had done with the class," she wailed. "He just tore strips off me in front of my children for the appearance of my work program."

Knowing him as I did, I would have prepared him before he went to her grade, but I had not been there.

"Go home Jodi, and don't return until you feel like it – probably that should be after the inspector finishes his inspection. I will see to it that you receive the credit you have richly deserved."

Hot on the heels of her leaving, the inspector stormed into the office.

"Where is that woman?" he roared.

"Half way home, on my recommendation. You really have no awareness of the feelings or needs of people, do you? Or if you have, it is obviously of no concern to you. Did you not notice her advanced pregnancy? If you had bothered to check objectively, you would have realised that, despite the work program wreck, she has taught exceptionally well. Now, because of your attitude towards her, either you or I will have to take that grade for the remainder of today. I suggest that it be you for long enough to report accurately and fairly on the quality of what has been achieved in that room."

"I don't need you to arrange my time table, and you were grossly remiss to accept that work program," was his final barb, as he once again stormed off.

To his considerable chagrin, I imagine, he struggled to unearth anything else at the school that really deserved criticism

As Murphy's Law decreed, two beneficial situations occurred around the middle of the year. They were welcome, but would have been of great assistance if they have arrived earlier. By the time they finally happened, I had nearly exhausted myself, but did have the school running smoothly, with the bus line transporting the children again, and having the children welcomed back into the interschool activity programs.

The first of these two new happenings occurred sometime in May. A knock at my office door heralded the arrival of a tiny, quietly spoken lady.

"Recently I moved to this area, and I would like to have some opportunities to do emergency teaching," she began.

I had been dreaming of this sort of thing happening for some time, as I badly needed someone to relieve me from teaching that Grade 6. However, I felt it was only fair to explain the situation to her. Realistically, if I just placed her in the Grade 6, they would probably gobble her up for a late breakfast and spit her out at morning recess.

"The Grade 6 needs a teacher right now, but this need is brought about by the fact that they are so difficult that no emergency teacher will take them," I explained with regretful honesty.

"Then your troubles and mine are both over," she whispered smilingly. "I'll teach them."

She was, however, so tiny and so quiet that I severely doubted the wisdom of the arrangement. Full of nervous premonition of an impending crisis, and remaining at the ready to be a Sir Gallahad, galloping up on a white stallion to save her, I let her loose on those predators.

What a surprise awaited me!

On her first day, she sat on the edge of a front desk, and spoke ever so softly to the dangerous pack. What she said must have been to their liking, as they leaned forward, silently, intently listening to her every word.

I was called away, but returned at the first opportunity, only to find every pupil working quietly and diligently. She obviously had them eating out of her hand and enjoying it. What a relief to find myself redundant!

All those many teachers who shout to gain attention, only managing to raise the classroom noise level even higher, should have the privilege of witnessing someone like her at work.

At the end of June, the second bonus occurred. Miracle of miracles, another man was appointed to the school, and not just another man. A relaxed and smiling person, he taught that Gr 6, easily maintaining strong discipline, while quickly achieving an excellent rapport with the children. As well, he was great company for me. With the pressure and responsibility no longer mine alone, it felt as if Christmas had come early.

The second half of the year progressed smoothly and was comparatively trouble free, except for one morning, when I arrived at school early, as was my habit and I saw a large hole in the school ground. The grounds were terraced and on one terrace I discovered a large, quite dangerous hole. After constructing a temporary fence around it and placing large signs of 'KEEP AWAY', I rang the school president.

"It has happened before," he calmly responded. "If you like I will contact the same contractors as on the last occasion. I'm sure they will regard it as a priority to make it safe for the children."

I did like, thankfully left it to him, and proceeded to appoint an extra member of staff to yard duty to ensure that safety in the meantime.

At the conclusion of that year, strange as it may seem, as it had been a constantly stressful time, I reluctantly left the school to regain my promotion. It was rather gratifying to me, though, that I could leave it in a far better state than it had been in when I had arrived.

****

Chapter 14

VICE PRINCIPAL AGAIN

True to form, the school to which I was appointed was classed as a disadvantaged school, due to the fact that a third of the children came from single parent homes or dysfunctional families. As Malcolm Fraser might have said, 'my teaching life was not meant to be easy'. It was a school of four hundred plus pupils, and I became one of its two vice principals. We had no classroom responsibility, but the other vice principal was already responsible for organising the teaching of reading and English throughout the school and administrating the upper school. The principal asked me to perform the same role with mathematics throughout the whole school, and organising the infant school department. This I found an interesting challenge, as, although I had taught infants in one-teacher schools, and had firm ideas of what skills I expected from children when they arrived in the upper school, I had never actually taught an infant grade. The two prep teachers wished to team-teach in a double room, so I decided to remedy my inexperience by making it a three-teacher team for part of each day. I loved every minute of my time with the children and learnt a lot.

In the past, I had found that many teachers were uncertain of how to teach the new mathematics course. Keeping this in mind, I rewrote the maths curriculum, including detailed information of not only the material to be taught, but also of how to present it, even including useful individual activity cards and other helpful aids. I emphasised the need of ensuring that each child progress at his or her own rate, and fully understand every process of each level before moving on. To ensure this I re-iterated the important principles of moving from the known to the unknown, the simple to the complex and from the concrete to the abstract, as expounded by Elijah and Cole. I also recommended techniques of assessing and recording progress. The teachers found it so useful that the principals of the two largest schools in the inspectorate requested permission to replace their courses with it word for word. Another local principal, who had just gained an appointment as inspector to a neighbouring district, took it with him to commend it to his schools.

Two most likeable middle-aged bachelors had taught the two Grade 5s of the school for twenty-five years, with their methods having changed little during that long period. Having enjoyed and benefitted from my infant teaching experience, I arranged for them to change grades the second year – one to a Grade 3 and the other to a Grade 2. They were mortified, particularly the one heading to Grade 2.

"I won't even know what to teach them let alone how to do it," he wailed.

"It need only be for one year if it doesn't suit you, Bob. Early in the year I will work with you until you are comfortable," I re-assured him.

As it eventuated, I was virtually redundant. He took to it like a duck to water. The children adored him and he soon learned to love them and the job in general. After dreading it initially he thanked me for forcing it on him.

"Best teaching move I ever made," he enthused.

At one stage of that year the principal was away and I had taken his place. While working at the office table one day I just managed to notice the figure of a large man stride purposefully past the open door. This is a real no-no in a school. Anyone wishing to go to a classroom must call at the office first. The wellbeing and safety of the children is a vital responsibility of a school, and the teachers must not be approached without the principal's permission.

Without a moment's hesitation, I rushed out to intercept him.

"Wait!" I called. "Where do you think you are going?"

"I'm heading to the Grade 2 room to knock that bloody teacher's head off," he snapped angrily.

"You're not, you know, because if you take one more step, I will have the police here in a flash."

As he hesitated, giving this unexpected development some thought, I suggested he first come to my office as the law decreed, and we would discuss his concern.

Grudgingly he complied.

"That teacher belted my kid over the ear. No-one does that to my kid and gets away with it." He was thoroughly incensed, and had to be calmed.

Knowing that gentle Bob could never do that to any child for any reason I suggested an alternative.

"All children sometimes stretch the truth a little," I said, making sure I couldn't be misconstrued as saying they tell lies. "I suggest that we get the teacher, you and your son into my office all together. I'm sure we will find out exactly what happened so none of us has to regret a hasty action later."

Not entirely comfortable with the arrangement he did agree.

It is not difficult to gain the truth from a child if you know how, and most teachers do. Without much persuasion, he admitted that he had made it all up to get some attention from his dad.

Now, highly embarrassed, and with his anger redirected, the father apologised to the teacher, but I was concerned that he might take his anger out now on the child, so I sent the teacher and boy back to the classroom and began to chat with him.

"I imagine you are a busy man," I began.

"If you have kids to raise, you have to be," he responded. "Could I tell you a very brief story?" I asked. He agreed, so I continued. "When my kids were the same age as your lad, my wife told me that I was being a wonderful teacher and very active community member, but at the expense of time with my kids. We had a young bloke boarding with us and she added that he spent more time with them than I did. It shocked me as I realised that, though I previously hadn't noticed it, she was quite correct. Obviously, this couldn't continue, so I immediately applied for a job on an island to get away from community demands and spend more time doing things with my family. I have been rewarded for it ever since. Do you think your lad is, in a funny way, trying to give you a similar message?"

After a moment of thought, he replied, "Perhaps he is, but it was a bloody stupid way to do it."

Obviously, I hadn't quite won yet, but it was a start worth pursuing.

"We know that, but kids of his age sometimes can't think of a better way. If you would accept a suggestion, I feel that punishment would make the situation worse. Make him understand that he was wrong by all means, but if you can find some time to spend with him, I doubt it would happen again."

With fingers crossed that I had got through to him, I showed him out.

****

CHAPTER 15

A LECTURER

During one year, I received an SOS from the Education Faculty at a University. The final year primary education students were threatening to go on strike. Apparently, their complaint was that they had done three and a half years of useless advanced tertiary maths, and were due to become teachers in six months, but had no idea how to teach primary maths to children.

To me this reflected badly on their lecturers and course content. Sometimes it would seem some of these lecturers have been away from the coalface too long.

Would I become an associate lecturer, and conduct a six-month course on the practical teaching of maths of an evening?

Despite begrudging the time, I felt it was important, so agreed.

At the beginning of our first session I surveyed the sea of eager young faces that reminded me of fledglings in a nest waiting open-mouthed, to be fed. Lectures from me with unquestioned acceptance from them was most certainly not what I wanted. Two-way communication, with questions and comments from them would be far more productive and enjoyable. I made a snap decision to change tack and shock them, to ensure that they became active participants and contributed to their learning process. The last thing I wanted was to lecture to a passive audience.

"You must remember that you are teaching children, not babies, so don't baby them, or give them work they find easy!" I thundered in my most authoritative voice. "They need to be constantly challenged by tasks they have to struggle to complete. School is not meant to be

fun. If a child is smiling, you haven't kept him or her sufficiently busy."
Continuing in that way for a bit longer I was hoping to be challenged
by someone, but no challenge was forthcoming. Some were even taking
notes.

With hardly a pause for breath, I continued, "You people have
listened passively to a load of total crap. You have had seven years of
primary education, six years of secondary education and three and a
half years of an education degree, and you are sitting there passively
accepting that utter nonsense?" I scornfully rebuked them.

"Did it really make sense to you?" I finally asked.

"I thought the smiling part was a bit harsh," one person hesitantly
offered.

"Well, thank goodness for that, at least. For heaven's sake!

"Move from the Known to the Unknown.

You have just accepted a pile of ridiculous rot, because I am supposed to be an authority. If these sessions are to be worthwhile you must listen, consider carefully what you have heard, and ask questions if you need any clarification or have any doubts. Perhaps you might want to disagree with some point, or make some suggestion. With discussion, we might even find a better solution. Contributions from you will not just be okay, but most welcome, in fact, necessary to the success of this course. A teacher I had in year 11 changed me from a student who just scraped a pass in maths to one who didn't have to sit final internal exams because he had scored such high marks during the year. He was a fearsome man named Bill Woodful, and happened to have been the captain of the Australian Test Cricket team before Don Bradman.

'You will excel in maths this year, or else you will answer to me' he roared in awesome tones. 'You will succeed because if there is any slight doubt in your mind, you will ask me to clarify that matter, until you totally understand.'

I will bet no team member under him stepped out of line. We certainly didn't.

To learn you must listen to, or read, lots of information, but most of what you take in is opinion, rather than irrefutable fact. Take it in, then analyse it before you accept it. Maybe you need to modify it before accepting it.

I once had a Grade 4 boy raise his hand and hesitantly say, 'I think you are wrong, sir,' and yet you adults couldn't do that.

Now – perhaps the first lesson in being a teacher, before we concentrate specifically on maths, should be, what you think my re-action to that situation with the Grade 4 boy should have been?"

Thankfully, lively discussion followed, and continued for the duration of the lectures. When the Grade 4-boy situation had been thrashed out, I introduced the program with the following.

"What I spouted at the start was a total contradiction to the wonderful principles of teaching proposed by two men named Elijah and Cole, who were way ahead of their time when they wrote what they believed to be the principles of effective teaching in their text book. I studied their beliefs during my training, and would have hoped you might have done so too. It was true then, as it remains today, and will continue to be into the future, as long as you teach. If you haven't studied it, then write these three things down and make them your bible for teaching maths certainly, but not only maths. All teaching, should be based on them.

Start writing : -

Learning should proceed from the known to the unknown, from the simple to the complex, and from the concrete to the abstract. We will expand greatly on those three statements, but they will remain our guiding principles."

At last we were away and running. Although the lectures basically concentrated on maths, they wandered to every other facet of teaching, particularly, of course to my special enthusiasms of reading, English composition, physical education, singing and acting and contained a heavy emphasis on education being fun. The lectures were officially from 7.00pm to 9.00pm, but rarely could I close the doors behind them before midnight. Their thirst for knowledge about how best to teach children was almost unquenchable.

I gave to the faculty, a detailed report about the way the lectures progressed. I hope the powers that be, learnt from the experience, as their program was not producing confident competent teachers as it was.

****

CONCLUSION

It has been said that I can become overexcited at a sporting event. The following appears to support that statement. My son, Doug, had been training long and hard for a boatrace. He and the crew of which he was the stroke, deserved to do well. They had trained daily, beginning at 5.30am. Having become very well acquainted with them, as they, other than Doug, were all boarders at the school, and had virtually lived in our home, I was most proud of their dedication, and was very keen for them to succeed. Becoming rather carried away I barracked fanatically from the shore, resulting in the crew not only winning, but creating a new record that stood for ten years.

Although Doug claimed that they couldn't hear me at all out there on the lake, I claim some of the credit. Something of worth had to come from my efforts, because otherwise it was a disaster. I damaged my voice so severely that I was forced to retire from teaching at the tender age of forty-six, and from the singing and stage performing that I loved. Arguing that with my knowledge and experience, I had lots still to offer, I failed to convince the powers that be. Education Department red tape stated that if your voice did not allow you to teach all day, you had the choice of early retirement, or working as a clerk in the education offices in Melbourne on a clerk's wages. Red tape decrees are all-powerful in government departments, so I reluctantly retired.

Fortunately, I have been able to resurrect my teaching career in a small way, that of tutoring at the University of the Third Age. It is quite a change teaching people over fifty, but many of the principles remain the same, and it is still a most rewarding experience. Although I am critical of some things happening in present day education, I would like to acknowledge that there are some excellent things happening. I regularly attend Merrimac High School, where the principal has welcomed our U3A students to conduct our studies. The atmosphere, noticeable immediately you walk through the gate, assures that children who attend the school are indeed privileged.

To conclude this book, which has provided me with much satisfaction in the writing, perhaps I can summarize my philosophy of teaching in point form.

1. This I place first as I regard it as vital. Love the children you teach, enjoy your time with them, and make your enjoyment obvious. That last bit is probably quite redundant, as children, like dogs, are most perceptive of the genuineness of your emotions. The importance of this is that, if, and only if, it is genuine, the children will reciprocate, and both sides will benefit greatly. The children will co-operate and try to please, and their learning will be far more effective.

2. Prepare the yearly courses thoroughly and with carefully thought out detail, including your method of approach. If you clearly know where you need to go, you will be more effective. Prepare also for each week, sometimes a little longer ahead, and for each day. I have heard experienced teachers claim that with their knowledge of the courses and their experience in teaching them, that they can effectively wing it without preparation. They are right – you can, but afterwards you will always think of something you could have included or of some better approach you could have taken.

3. Be friendly, but firm. This is particularly important early in your relationship with your pupils. Friendly engenders co-operation and co-operation achieves much more than confrontation. By nature, though, children can take advantage of this approach, so the first sign of this must be firmly nipped in the bud. It is helpful at times to allow them some rope, but children must know how far they can stretch it. They enjoy knowing exactly where they stand and how far they can go.

4. Complementing number three, and vital to it, is consistency. What is right and allowed must be always allowed, but equally what is not must never be accepted. If children can sometimes get away with certain poor behaviour and sometimes not, they will often try it to see if this is one of the former.

5. At all times, be yourself. Children enjoy teachers who can laugh and show their feelings. Putting on a teacher persona is a counter-productive method, to which children will not respond. Laugh <u>with</u> children, and at yourself rather than <u>at</u> children. A child should never be embarrassed by your laughter. This leads to the next thought.

6. Make school fun for children. This can be achieved in many ways. No child should be frightened, so bullying must be eliminated. Bullying has always taken place and will always happen, but every effort should be made to prevent it. Emphasising the idea of everyone being happy is a start. Another way is starting a buddy system, where each of the older children become the friend of a younger child. I remembered that my own younger brother, whose nature was susceptible to being bullied, suffered it rarely, because he had an older brother at the school. This system benefits the older children too, as it makes them feel responsible, accountable and achieving. Teachers perform yard duty, which should involve far more than seeing that the grounds are kept tidy. By being observant, it is possible to see the possibilities of situations developing and preventing them from happening. Children love a teacher participating in their play, even if it is only for a moment or two. This can engender friendly rapport with them and creates a happy environment in which bullying does not thrive.

7. Make the classroom fun. Activities like rote repetition do not contribute well to fun. A little may be necessary, but even that can be done in novel ways that can be made fun. Learning via games and competitions certainly does. Important things like number facts and tables in maths lessons, and phonic and word recognition certainly can be both learned effectively via having fun through games and competitions. Activities like singing, planned and impromptu acting, and physical activities make great breaks from other lessons that require concentrated effort. Children cannot sit and concentrate for long periods of time, nor should they be expected to do so.

8. Be an interested listener. Look at and listen intently to a child who is speaking to you and respond encouragingly. Although

what he or she says may not always seem important to you, it surely will be to the child.

9. Recognition and reward are important, whether it be for high standards achieved, for improvement, for being dependable, or for something like a kind deed or thoughtful act. Praise from the teacher is often the best reward, with employing a classroom house points system an effective aid.

10. Every child must experience success, be it in academic subjects, sport, singing, acting, or even by being a good monitor.

11. As often as possible, broaden the experience of children by taking them beyond the school environment. At an early stage the children's reading will benefit from strolling around their local shopping centre reading all the signs. This activity also helps them to become fully aware of their environment. By studying The Merchant of Venice page by page, and dissecting it in the classroom, I learnt to hate Shakespeare, until I eventually saw his plays. How much better would it have been if my school had organised the chance to view it first, or even act some scenes.

12. Education should be based on the old principles preached by Elijah and Cole – that children should progress from the known to the unknown, from the simple to the complex and from the concrete to the abstract, to ensure both confidence and competence. However, children should often be challenged to keep them ambitious.

13. Pay special attention to helping your pupils to develop their memories. Regular memory competitions and games pay dividends

14. Your responsibility to children goes far beyond teaching them facts. It includes the development of the total child, personality, and character, including initiative, self-respect and self-confidence. Consideration and respect for others are also vital aspects. You should encourage a love of learning, teach children how to independently learn, and aim to broaden children's life experiences and their confidence in participating therein.

As a final comment, modern educational philosophy would no doubt frown on my use of corporal punishment. It is not for me to say whether it was right or wrong, and certainly it was at times misused by some teachers – maybe there are better ways.

Comments I would make though, are that it worked for me. The mother of a child whom I had recently strapped, came to me once and said,

"Harry thinks the sun, moon, and stars shine out of you."

I laughed and said, "And I have just recently strapped him."

He was a 'fighting cock', and would fight anyone of any age. When the most recent fight was with a younger boy, it had to be construed as bullying, even though to him it was probably just another fight.

"Knowing Harry, he would have fully deserved it, and probably would have been disappointed if he had got away scot free, indicating that you didn't care enough about him to give him the punishment he deserved," she quickly responded.

I may explain that I used the strap only on rare occasions, but the children knew it was an option if deserved. Mainly it was used for bullying, occasionally for rank defiance of one of my teachers. If I had relied on corporal punishment alone for discipline, or if I had ever delivered it in anger, I should certainly be rightfully criticised. Along with it, I employed such techniques as setting clear standards with the reasons for them. I readily gave affection and showed genuine interest in all pupils, placing co-operation before confrontation, being generous with praise when it was deserved, and encouraging pride in themselves and in their school. Always I emphasised that along with their own rights, the rights of others should be respected.

Whether I chose the best course of action or not, it seemed to work for me. Bullying was rare in my schools, achievement was high, with very few children leaving the school unable to read, and most children enjoyed their school life. They also left school with far more respect and consideration for others in the community than I see evident today. Many have become personal friends in later years, and several remain so today.

An observation.

A disturbing number of children are expelled or suspended from school, and bullying prevails in both schools and the community. Community literacy standards remain too low, and many in the community don't participate in sport or some form of exercise. While these situations prevail, and there is violence, both general and domestic, in our community, and, as long as people turn to drugs, indicating that they are unhappy with who they are, and want to escape their situation, then, despite some excellent outcomes, our education system remains flawed.

Thus, we need to continue in our efforts to seek ways to improve how we educate our children, and how we train our teachers. Having benefitted from the practical learning of the student teaching program, which meant that theory had clearer meaning when we progressed to studying it, I personally would love to see teacher training returning to that format.

Successful improvement of our education program requires thoughtful input from teachers, parents, administrators and politicians. I mention the politicians, as recently they have cut funding to universities, particularly in the cultural courses. How short-sighted! Imagine communities with no music, art, drama, and dancing.

****

I respectfully suggest that all teachers, particularly young teachers, make the time and effort to clearly formulate their own philosophy of teaching within acceptable guidelines. Doing so certainly aided me in delivering to the best of my ability.

****

Printed in the United States
By Bookmasters